OPEN BORDERS

A Personal Story of Love, Loss and Anti-War Activism

Betsy Bell

And

Four Personal Accounts of Citizen Diplomacy in the 1980s

By
Roscius Doan
Craig Justice
Anne Stadler
Dick Carter

Kenmore, WA

Epicenter Press

Epicenter Press is a regional press publishing nonfiction books about the arts, history, environment, and diverse cultures and lifestyles of Alaska and the Pacific Northwest.

For more information, visit www.EpicenterPress.com

This is a work of nonfiction. Real names have been used with permission, others have been changed.

ISBN: 978-1-941890-21-9 (Trade Paperback)
ISBN: 978-1-941890-23-3 (Ebook)

Library of Congress Control Number: 2018954455

Printed in the United States of America

For Don

Contents

INTRODUCTION

Thirty-five years ago, citizens in Seattle stepped up to the threat of nuclear destruction by pushing the Cold War borders open. Leaders, including my husband, Aldon Bell (Don) organized around a belief that ordinary people could influence governments to settle conflict through diplomacy rather than war. They insisted on travel and trade between enemy superpowers.

This period in Seattle's history coincided with my own personal efforts to open the constraining borders of my career and my marriage. Throughout my long partnership with Don, I struggled to shed my role as student, never sure of my particular value in our relationship. He had been my teacher when I was seventeen.

Through the examination of a period of intense political activity in my life, I have been able to trace my passage to independence. Mine is the story of many women born during World War II and raised at a time when the prevailing expectation of women in America was that they would marry, raise children, and be a supportive wife. In spite of my parents' encouragement—they sent me off on teenage adventures— and their challenge that I could do anything I wanted in life, the fifties' model of a supportive wife to which both Don and I aspired curbed my independence.

Open Borders is an account of my small role in the anti-nuclear war efforts from 1982-1984 called Target Seattle and Target Washington and the years of continued cultural exchanges with the USSR up to 1990. Hundreds of other Seattleites and ordinary citizens across the country have stories to tell about their friendships across the Iron Curtain that separated Russia and its eastern block of Soviet Socialist Republics from the United States and her allies in western Europe.

After traveling to the Soviet Union to carry letters of peace to

Seattle's Sister City, Tashkent in Uzbekistan in March of 1983, I became obsessed with helping our photographer create a multimedia slide show. I believed its message of love would convince politicians to change their approach to the arms race.

Four friends who were involved in such efforts have granted me permission to include an essay by each of them documenting how their life and work were affected by the anti-nuclear war efforts.

Writing Open Borders made me realize how proud I am of the many people who worked so hard in the 1980s to prevent nuclear war. We embraced our so-called enemies with curiosity, compassion, respect, and the firm belief that we all shared the common values of love of place and love of family. Nuclear war was not an option for us ordinary people. It would destroy all we hold dear.

Today, I am more frightened by the possibility of nuclear war than I was in 1982. I also feel alone. If there are others trembling before the "fire and fury" rhetoric and the repeating rocket and hydrogen tests, I hope this story of our activism will stir them to find ways to organize, to seek peace through cross-border understandings of our common humanity and the love we each have for our homeland.

Why does it seem so few are alarmed at the threat of nuclear war today? Are we in denial or overwhelmed by the enormity of so many doomsday crises at once? Or have we, as I worry, left behind as antiquated that practice humans have engaged in for millennia of gathering in groups to work things out with minds firmly connected to hearts? Eye to eye conversations are much more effective than thumbs tapping through electronic devices. Through the latter half of the 20th century, as much as the Kremlin in Russia and the White House disagreed with how our world should be organized, one felt the leaders grasped their sober responsibility for the future of the whole world and genuinely did not want to put all that fire power to use. Today, I am not so sure. Putting words on paper is my way of taking up arms again. Action gives me hope.

Seattle and Tashkent in Uzbekistan had have a long-standing sister city relationship. Using that entrée into the Soviet Union, our Target Seattle group modeled an ever-increasing flood of people-to-people exchanges across the Iron Curtain. These exchanges created friendships between ordinary people. Did these friendships contribute to the collapse of the Berlin Wall? Perhaps. Will what we did in the 80s influence a new generation to befriend those whom our government vilifies and thereby slow down, or even reverse the threat of nuclear destruction? I hope so.

Open Borders

Thirty-five years ago, many speculated that if a nuclear war broke out, Seattle would be a primary target. The specter of a Hiroshima-style wasteland where Puget Sound lies caused local panic. The Cuban Missile Crisis in 1962 had elevated the level of fear. The Cold War simmered through the Vietnam War years and tensions with the Soviets roller-coastered through the Carter presidency. By the eighties, nuclear submarines were stationed on the Kitsap Peninsula, only a ferry ride away from Seattle. Under Reagan, military spending shot up even while the president's team engaged in negotiating a treaty to slow the madness. Children in Seattle schools rehearsed duck-and-cover bomb drills under their desks. Three sun-yellow upside-down triangles appeared on any building strong enough to serve as a fallout shelter. A troupe of actors staged *Four Minutes to Midnight* with a clock ticking that sent chills down my spine. White chalk outlines to simulate vaporized bodies appeared on Seattle sidewalks. Nike missiles encircled the city.

Not everyone cringed in silence. A group of ordinary citizens decided to see what could be done to prevent nuclear war. On March 20, 1983, the same year President Reagan called the Soviet Union an evil empire, I traveled to the Soviet Union with my husband, Aldon (Don) Bell, our seventeen-year-old daughter, Ruth, and thirty other Seattleites. We had a letter to deliver, a request that people in our sister city, Tashkent, capital of the Soviet Republic of Uzbekistan join us to work to prevent nuclear war.

That remarkable trip would change my life forever, and not all for the better.

DON LOOKED UP FROM HIS suitcase, went to his desk at the office end

1

of our twenty-five-foot-long master bedroom and came back to face me, holding two pieces of paper in his hand. It was late the night before we were to fly from Seattle to Helsinki, then on to Moscow, Tashkent, Samarkand, and Leningrad (St. Petersburg) to deliver the peace letters to people in our sister city, Tashkent. I had just set the packet of peace letters on top of the folded shirts in our suitcases.

"Betsy," the hollow sound of his voice worried me. "I can't decide what to do about these letters."

"Letters? What letters? Different from these peace petitions?" I pointed to the suitcase.

"Letters to two families, Jews, living in Moscow. They are refuseniks."

Refuseniks were people denied permission to leave the Soviet Union. Nearly all of them were Jews hoping to emigrate to Israel. They had become Cold-War pawns, allowed to leave when the Kremlin needed good publicity and refused when anger at the West was strongest. The new leader in Moscow, Yuri Andropov, a ruthless former head of the KGB, was particularly harsh against dissidents and Jews who sought exit visas. The Soviet Union's invasion of Afghanistan and President Carter's withdrawal of US athletes from the 1980 Olympics in Moscow had made things more precarious for the refuseniks. This was a bad time for anyone who tried to help, and a worse time for them. Human Rights Watch was calling attention to their terrible plight. They were labeled traitors to the state, were not allowed to work, to participate in international events in their field, or to move freely about the country. At a Target Seattle planning meeting, we'd talked about the refuseniks. We'd even done role-playing exercises so that none of us traveling to the USSR would be coaxed into criticizing the Soviets for their treatment of the refuseniks, or anything else.

I must have asked Don where he got the letters, but I don't remember his answer. What I do remember is how important it suddenly felt to me that we bring them. And the anger I felt that only then was he including me in the decision.

"Why are you only just telling me about these tonight?"

"I've been weighing the risk of carrying them with us and getting caught with them. I wouldn't have even considered taking them but I know how much you care about the refusenik situation," Don said.

My uncle Tom had first made me aware of the refuseniks. When

I was a freshman at Bryn Mawr College I visited him at his home in Georgetown, Maryland, a short train ride from Bryn Mawr. Tom was chairman of Raytheon's atomic and nuclear energy research department. We talked about the scientists he had worked with, including Jews Leo Szilard and Edward Teller, at the Brookhaven National Laboratory. Tom had been very upset when Senator McCarthy went on a witch hunt for communists, including some of his colleagues. Recently, Tom and I had talked about the refuseniks by phone. Tom was in his nineties and still passionate about never using nuclear power for making war.

"Of course, we have to take them," I said.

"I knew you'd say that. They could get us all kicked out."

"I want to take them. For Uncle Tom's sake." I glared at Don. "It's worth the risk."

"I'm not so sure." He studied the letters, folding and unfolding them. "Are you really willing to put everyone else on the trip at risk? What about all the people who've put their hope in us?" He pointed to the bundles of letters. "If these two refusenik letters were discovered, the whole group could get sent home without ever getting to Uzbekistan."

Ordinarily I was cautious about stepping too far out of Don's comfort zone, but I felt a wellspring of passion. I took his hand in mine. "We won't get caught. You're clever. You'll think of a way to hide these two letters. We'll show the packets of friendship letters as we go through customs and at every official meeting. No one will suspect two hidden letters."

"Tom's upset that Russian Jewish scientists can't participate in international scientific meetings," Don said. "These two families probably have nothing to do with science."

"Don, they're human beings. We're taking those letters. Isn't that what this whole thing is about? Forging human connections. It's the right thing to do. Now figure it out."

Shaking, I stormed out of the room.

When I first met Don, I was only seventeen. He'd come to Muskogee, Oklahoma, via Oxford, England. His Texas draft board had called him home, then left him hanging with nothing to do. Killing time, he took a job as a substitute teacher of history at my high school. He was only twenty-three, five and a half years my senior. He'd already finished college, and three additional years as a Rhodes scholar. He was refined and worldly compared to the other boys I'd dated. I fell in love with his mind, his shyness, and the way he stood up to my domineering father.

After Don fulfilled his army obligation, we married. I'd just finished my sophomore year in college. While I completed my bachelor of arts degree, he finished his PhD. I'd just given birth to Grace, our first child, when the University of Kansas offered Don his first real teaching job. We moved to Lawrence, Kansas, and settled into our first home. While he taught, I worked on my master's degree in Spanish Literature. Don wanted lots of children and I wasn't averse to the idea. Priscilla was born next and while the children and the house kept me busy, I somehow managed to finish the master's degree. Before Eleanor, our third, was born, I began a teaching career. By the time I was pregnant with Ruth, I was teaching part time at the University of Kansas and volunteering in support of women's reproductive rights. Life was busy but good.

Then Don took the job at the University of Washington as Dean of Undergraduate and Interdisciplinary Education and we moved to Seattle. I gave up teaching and the volunteer work I loved. My role, I believed, was to support Don.

Sitting in the hallway fuming about Don's hesitation to support my concern for the refuseniks made me feel weak. He'd been my teacher when I met him and in many ways, he still was. I learned from him and that emboldened me, but always within limits. His limits.

When I walked back into the room, Don had emptied his camera bag onto the bed and was rummaging through the contents. "Maybe we can hide the letters by rolling them into empty film canisters." He folded, then wound one of the letters and slid it into a canister.

"This will work. Two canisters in Marlow's camera bag should go unnoticed. The whole group doesn't need to know about them. Or any of this, for that matter."

I smiled and cocked my head. Don was like Ben Franklin, the nimble negotiator, working any difficult situation by appealing to the feelings of adversary and ally alike. I was the Sam Adams, tossing tea into the harbor in protest. I reached up and planted a kiss on his lips. "I knew you'd figure something out."

Marlow Boyer, whose camera bag the letters would be hidden in, was the talented son of a *National Geographic* photographer and a student at the University of Washington. Don had interviewed Marlow as an applicant for the Rhodes scholarship and was disappointed when he didn't win the nomination. He was impressed with Marlow's resume and asked him to be our official photographer. I knew Marlow would be excited about the cloak-and-dagger intrigue.

It was nearly midnight by the time we settled ourselves in bed, hoping for some sleep.

Looking back on the incident, I realized Don and I accepted those letters without knowing their content. Neither of us could read Russian. My own enthusiasm for breaking down barriers between people propelled me forward, headlong. I later learned about a man who went to Moscow determined to visit a refusenik family. When he got to the address, the numbers had been painted out. That night, a couple of KGB agents knocked on his hotel door, woke him out of a sound sleep, and interrogated him. Perhaps knowing about this incident would have cooled my ardor for taking the letters. But I don't think so.

I drifted off to sleep wondering how we were going to get away with handing out letters of peace to people on the street. Never mind the extra two secret letters to refuseniks.

When morning came, I wandered around the garden to calm myself. Don had planted dozens of crocuses and daffodils. Yellow and purple dotted the front yard. His early peas were up and there were neat rows of lettuce seeds with their markers. He planted. I harvested, complaining about the density of growth in his tiny patch of rich soil. Nowhere to put my feet. Pruning the overgrown front yard gave me pleasure; chopping out the dead wood from the too-cheerful *Autumnalis*. Its lavish January blooms were gone. Year after year, those airy clouds seemed to mock the gray gloom of the Northwest winter and what I left behind in Kansas. But I did love living where the only thing keeping me from the outdoors was inadequate clothing—never too hot or too cold. Nothing could persuade me to turn the clock back, but with the kids growing up I longed for more. Maybe this adventure to the USSR would open a new world for me.

THE WHOLE ADVENTURE WAS BORN one night in the early winter of 1982. Don announced that he was going to a meeting at the home of one of Seattle's most engaged civic leaders, Kay Bullitt, to plan a local response to the doctrine of peace through strength. If Seattle is a target, what could we do to prevent the bombs from falling? Leaders with Physicians for Social Responsibility, Ploughshares (former Peace Corps volunteers), the international YMCA, KING-TV5 station (owned by Kay's mother-in-law, Dorothy Bullitt), and lawyers from the progressive firm of McDonald Hogue & Bayless, were among those gathered and ready to act. A ten-day series of educational events called *Target Seattle: Preventing Nuclear War* came out of that meeting and the many that followed. A couple of these leaders would be on the plane with us heading for the USSR. The organizers chose Don to chair the planning and execution of the ten-day program on the growing threat of nuclear war and what such a conflagration would mean for Seattle and Western Washington. While dean of Continuing Education at the University of Washington and associate professor of History, he had spearheaded the university and business communities' anti-apartheid divestment efforts in the late seventies. He was a good choice for the task of leading Target Seattle.

The pressures on his time and planning skills spilled into our life at home, but despite the stresses, I supported his commitment. Both Don and I believed our progressive Episcopal faith tradition urged us on as change agents for a more interconnected world. Don's role as Target Seattle's leader compelled him more than his university administrative duties. He told the provost he would be traveling to Russia during spring break; he did not ask permission.

At the time, I worked part time at Saint Mark's Cathedral as a member of the program staff that worked for Cabby Tennis, the cathedral's dean. Dean Cabell Tennis supported the antinuclear effort and encouraged me to organize and manage seminars, forums, and classes related to Target Seattle. A highlight was hosting the *Four Minutes to Midnight* players and a discussion of the nuclear crisis. The cathedral was known for progressive stands on racial, homelessness, and other social justice issues, which made it a natural fit for many other Target Seattle planning meetings and events.

Target Seattle teach-ins attracted thousands of Seattleites. It was encouraging to listen to the constructive thinking of people like Archibald Cox, Linus Pauling, and Dr. Helen Caldicott, the head of Physicians for Social Responsibility. Four women, Ann Stadler,

Virginia McDermott, Lucy Dougall and Kathleen Braden, wrote a letter asking people in Seattle's sister city, Tashkent in Uzbekistan, to join us in working to prevent nuclear war. The peace letter said:

> The people of Seattle and Tashkent are united through the Sister City Program, through our love for our cities, and through the hopes we share for our children's futures. Yet if there is a nuclear war, all that we value would be destroyed …. We must work together to create peaceful means of resolving conflicts and take steps to reduce the danger of nuclear war.

The people of Seattle and Tashkent a
Жители Сиэтла и Ташкента, побратимов-гор
City Program, through our love for o
своим городам и взаимными надеждами на с
hopes we share for our children's futu
детей. Мы понимаем, что в случае ядерно
nuclear war, all that we value would k
дорожим, будет уничтожено. Как представи
who live in the Puget Sound commun

The committee printed hundreds of 8½" x 14" copies of this note, Cyrillic letters running beneath English, leaving room for signatures at the bottom. Organizers carried these letters to Target Seattle teach-ins, schools, and churches, and at the final event when twenty thousand people gathered in the Kingdome. Forty-two thousand people— Seattleites who feared our planet would be blown to smithereens by the Soviets or the Americans—signed them. Each person penned his or her name with the hope that someone like themselves living in Tashkent would read the letter. Grade-school children signed in block letters and added drawings in the margins—peace signs and mushroom clouds. One first-grade child told her teacher she wasn't afraid of bombs dropping on her school because her daddy went to meetings every week to stop them.

When the Target Seattle events ended, the committee called a meeting to decide how to get these letters to real people on the other side of the Iron Curtain. At the bottom of each one was printed the promise *This letter will be sent to Seattle's Russian sister city, Tashkent, and to government officials of the Soviet Union and the United States.* We laughed when we talked about mailing them, imagining the boxed-up letters sitting on the mayor of Tashkent's desk, how he'd marvel at the sentimentality of Americans as his colleagues looked over his shoulder. Then, we figured, he'd throw the whole mess in a dumpster behind the office buildings. That is, if the boxes ever got to Uzbekistan.

After an attempt failed to have other travelers to Tashkent take the letters, Virginia McDermott suggested we take them ourselves. It was a lark, an adventure. An invitation went out to people who might want to make the trip. Dick Blount's Holiday House travel agency worked out the travel details. Don and Virginia agreed to be the leaders. We began training ourselves to be bearers of peace letters at a time of heightened nuclear threats. Experts in Soviet-US relations talked to the group of travelers. Each of us agreed to rules of conduct. The trip was no ordinary vacation. Carrying printed materials with the intent of distributing them in the Soviet Union carried risk. Official letters were sent in advance to Moscow's Peace Committee and Tashkent's mayor describing our intent. In spite of these preparations, some of us wondered if we could be interrogated and the letters confiscated. We hoped there would be safety in numbers.

GRACE, THE ELDEST OF OUR four daughters, was taking a break from college and drove us to the airport. "Don't plan on me picking you up when you get back. I'm meeting the NOAA research ship in Hawaii. I got the ordinary seaman job," she told us as she unloaded our bags. Our second daughter, Priscilla, was working in Florida; Eleanor, next in line, was in college back east. Ruth stood close to Don, and watched the three other young people, Nick, Sara, and Stam, coming with us say goodbye to their families. Several reporters took pictures and statements from Don and Virginia. The three of us boarded our flight with the others amid an air of nervous excitement, hugs, and calls of "good luck!"

It was impossible then to fly directly from the US to any city in the USSR. Our Washington State senator, Henry "Scoop" Jackson, was a staunch defender of peace through strength. His Jackson-Vanik Amendment to the US-Soviet Trade Reform Act linked the trade benefits Moscow wanted (most-favored-nation treatment for Soviet exports and US credits) to the exodus of Soviet Jews, a punishment from Congress for the Communist government's anti-Semitic crackdown on Jewish dissidents. In my mind, the Jackson-Vanik Amendment became a symbol of closed borders, along with the Berlin Wall.

During much of the flight, Don stood in the aisle with Virginia and a couple of others to role-play responses to possible scenarios we'd encounter once we landed. Even university experts on Soviet affairs couldn't give us much advice on how Yuri Andropov might influence the kind of reception we would receive. Andropov replaced Brezhnev as General Secretary of the Soviet Union in 1982. Would Andropov's reputation for handling the refuseniks harshly make our upcoming visit with the Soviet Peace Committee more nerve-racking? Our group appointment with Yuri Zhukov, chairman of the Soviet Peace Committee was the first official event of our stay in Moscow. Zhukov had served as chair of the State Committee for Cultural Relations with foreign countries in the 1950s and sixties and had hosted President Nixon in 1959. The Nuclear Freeze Campaign and the Unilateral Disarmament groups had sat down with him in the weeks before our moment in his chambers. He knew Americans, probably understood English. Still, how much did the change in the top leadership influence his reception of us?

A key member of our team was Masha Reichert, a student at the Jackson School who had studied in Russia and spoke the language fluently. She would be our unofficial translator, and would try to read body language and expressions to get a sense of how we were being treated.

When our plane landed in Helsinki, we moved through security and onto an Aeroflot plane without delay. The Russian-built plane shuddered as it took off. My seat was broken, the upholstery worn. The bunched-up aisle carpet showed metal flooring in places. I imagined the flight attendants catching their heels in the frayed carpet runner, sending trays of food and drink flying. Soviet citizens in heavy coats, fur hats, wool scarves, high boots, and gloves sat in silence. They carried string bags of vegetables and lumpy packages tied with newspaper and twine. Don looked over notes and leaned across the aisle to talk to Masha. Then, in the darkness of Russia's late afternoon, the wheels hit the Moscow runway. We walked out of the plane, down a metal staircase, and across wet tarmac to the Sheremetyevo International Airport to collect our luggage and go through customs.

Our group, silent and weary, lined up behind Don. Would the officials be upset by the packets of peace letters? How would they react? Every one of us had to surrender our passports. As I handed mine over, I felt naked, exposed, untethered to my homeland, a panic rising in my gut. We stood waiting for the luggage inspection hoping they would return our passports.

Don faced a young Soviet official across the luggage inspection belt and caught his eye. The man noticed the slim volume of Alexander Pushkin's poetry tucked under Don's arm. In heavily-accented English, he asked, "You like Pushkin?" Don nodded, smiled, and tucked his chin. The official said, "I like Ray Bradbury." Both men grinned broadly, eyes dancing. Those of us within earshot exhaled. The inspector unzipped the suitcase, picked up the manila envelope, and, eyebrows knit questioningly, held the envelope out to Don.

"May I?" Don asked. He removed a letter from the envelope. "Please, read it." He handed the letter to the customs official.

The official's eyes followed the Cyrillic letters across the page. *We pledge ourselves to work to prevent nuclear war.* A big grin spread across his face as he handed the letter back to Don and waved us through.

Next, the official unzipped Marlow's bag, removed and turned each lens in his hand, looked into the barrel of the camera, and opened the camera's back, empty of film. He kept one eye on Marlow's cherubic face capped with thick, wavy, dark hair. Marlow remained placid, whatever nerves may have jangled behind those inquisitive eyes. The inspector lifted several film canisters, shaking each one, then zipped the camera bag shut and pushed it along the counter. The two canisters with letters to the refuseniks escaped notice.

The officials returned our passports to us, and all thirty-three of us smiled, repressing whoops and hollers, as we walked outside and the airport doors closed behind us.

I was a little startled when Don and Virginia were whisked away in a Mercedes while the rest of us boarded a large tour bus. I peered anxiously through curtained windows as we rode through the sparsely populated district of Molzhaninovsky, then crossed the Moscow canal to the Ostankinsky District, where the stately Ostankino eighteenth-century palace contrasted with the Exhibition of Achievements of the National Economy, one of the largest exhibitions centers, museums and recreation complexes in the world, and the modernistic Ostankino Tower, the tallest structure in Europe.

After a thirty-five kilometer ride the bus approached a towering, futuristic-looking hotel, the Cosmos, situated on a rise just north of the center of Moscow. We pulled into the hotel's circular drive, in the center of which a space-age rocket swirled skyward in a burnished-metal arc. The Seattle travelers descended from the overheated bus into the brisk night air and entered the marble foyer, gazing somewhat incredulously at the vast reception hall with its wraparound balcony and inverted, bronze fixtures that flooded the ceiling with soft light. The black Mercedes with Don and Virginia pulled up at the front entrance hall. The driver opened the car door for them.

Don and Virginia enjoyed their own privileged check-in and private dining with the official Soviet hosts while I joined a couple of the single women at dinner in the main hotel dining room. I hugged Ruth as she and Sara Fleming, her roommate on the trip, disappeared into their room, whispering something about checking out the hotel night life with the three "boys" in our group. Don found our room and marveled about the exclusive treatment he and Virginia enjoyed as leaders. I confessed to being content to let them have the limelight. I much preferred to travel as an ordinary tourist. We collapsed into bed.

I hardly slept that first night. At dawn, I got up and walked to the window to peer out the curtains. White-headed ravens cawed from the stone windowsills four floors above the frozen March earth. The front drive was now covered in a thin blanket of snow. Beneath a flat, steel-gray sky, a lone man ran beside the hotel in a private, wooded garden. I wished I'd brought my running shoes, but suspected the track was exclusive to members of some inner circle.

After Don woke up, we joined our groggy group downstairs in the hotel for breakfast before our planned visit to the Soviet Peace Committee. The smell of burned coffee and the sulfurous odor of overcooked eggs suppressed hunger until, one by one, we discovered the buffet of *kolbasa* sausage and blinis, and *syrniki*, fried quark pancakes with sour cream, jam, and honey toppings. The drafty room had no decoration other than large black silhouettes of Lenin and red hammer and sickle cutouts. Fluorescent lights cast an institutional pall over our hunched shoulders. Between bites, we wrapped our arms in self-warming hugs. As the coffee and food reenergized us, conversations swelled to laughter, and exclamations about drippy faucets, ceiling tiles from which contraband Playboy magazines tumbled, and the sleep-defying caws of the white-mantled ravens. We were in Moscow, behind the Iron Curtain.

Soon, Vladimir, our tour guide and official translator, strode in and announced our bus would be ready to depart in thirty minutes. We finished up, then walked outside to a flat gray sky that threatened snow. The Soviet Peace Committee's offices at Thirty-Six Prospekt Mira were twenty minutes down the nearly empty boulevard (save for the occasional black Mercedes hiding some important person behind tinted windows).

We were ushered into a six-story gray stone building, up a wide staircase, and into a hallway lined with metal folding chairs. The scent of disinfectant mingled with the aroma of strong tea, which emanated from an enormous samovar at one end.

It was our turn to meet Yuri Zhukov, the chair of the Soviet Peace Committee. He and his subordinates stood to welcome us the way a school principal greets naughty children sent by an exasperated teacher. It was this meeting that worried Herbert Ellison, head of the Jackson School at the University of Washington. He had told Don we were tilting at windmills and might undermine the official Strategic Arms Reduction Treaty (START) negotiations between the USSR and the US toward warhead parity, led by General Edward Rowney. The US State Department had not been happy to grant us travel visas but agreed to do so since we claimed tourist status.

As we filed in, Vladimir guided Virginia and Don to the head table. Masha took a seat next to Don. Ruth and I joined the others along the sides of the open horseshoe table. I was dry-mouthed and nervous for Don. I picked up the headset in front of my place, poured myself a glass of water from one of the carafes and took a sip. My stomach tightened when I heard Chairman Zhukov's first question.

"Do you speak for your government?"

Choosing his words carefully, speaking slowly so the simultaneous translation could follow, Don answered, "We are a group of private citizens from Seattle, Washington, en route to visit our sister city, Tashkent. Our objective is to deliver copies of a friendship letter signed by our citizens, intended for the people of Tashkent."

Don kept eye contact with Masha, checking to see if the translation was accurate. He then handed a copy of the letter to the chairman, who read it quickly. The rigid set of Zhukov's mouth and deep frown relaxed just a little. Then with a quick pass of the letter to his assistant, his ominous composure reassembled itself. The chairman's next words parroted the official party line.

"Because of the vigorous and consistent efforts of the Communist Party of the Soviet Union toward peace, détente and disarmament in international relations have blazed a trail toward fruitful cooperation among peoples. As long as the imperialist threat led by the United States continues, the Soviet Union would have to protect itself."

His words, lacking conviction, sounded like an often-repeated soundtrack. Still, they thrust knife blades into my chest. Others winced as the translation came through.

Don took the floor again. He said that we in Seattle hoped for exchanges of students, of artists, of dancers, of athletes, so that ordinary people from both countries could work creatively together. Zhukov paused. He may have expected a message similar to the Nuclear Freeze Campaign and the Unilateral Disarmament supporters, groups openly hostile to the US government's peace-through-strength policy, groups whose representatives had already spoken to Zhukov.

He finally spoke. "The Soviet Union will never be the first to drop a bomb. The future of the human race depends on the president of the United States."

Don thanked him for his time. After much handshaking and flat-lipped smiles, we filed out. Outside, we boarded our bus, huddling together, trying to interpret the sense of the meeting. Don told us that Zhukov's lack of comment on the peace letters seemed to be a tacit permission to take them to Tashkent.

One from our group later translated the banner over the Peace Committee's head table: "There is no more important task than stopping the instigators of a new war. This is in the interests of all nations. U. V. Andropov."

We represented the villains on the other side of the ocean whether we wanted to play the role or not. Had Don's remarks tempered Zhukov's opinion? I was so proud of his ability to find words that could not be used to pigeonhole our group. We wanted friendship and the common goal of no bombs. It was a huge relief to be done with this necessary official visit.

The urgency of the nuclear protest receded as the we Seattleites were deposited at Voskresenskiye gate, just fifteen minutes from the Peace Committee offices. At the end of Red Square's uphill expanse of white paving stones—three football fields in length—stood Saint Basil's Cathedral. Its onion domes, like a confectioner's triumph in a kaleidoscope of color and decoration more whimsical than any picture, slowed the travelers, who walked arm in arm scattering, pausing, transfixed. To the right ran the coal-red crenelated wall of the Kremlin, its palace towers a looming backdrop for the low-lying tomb of Lenin.

A line of visitors stood waiting their turn to pay reverence to Communism's greatest icon. Directly opposite the mausoleum, on the eastern side of the square, lay the building which housed Russia's most famous shopping mall—the State Department Store, GUM. There was time to slip inside both the cathedral and the department store. In the first, no functional religion was allowed, but a couple of workers quietly applied new gold leaf to the worn altar decorations; in the second, little merchandise was available to purchase. It was whispered that on the third floor of the magnificent vaulted building, privileged card-carrying people could buy anything Europe had to offer.

People scattered for dinner, some to Masha's Russian friends from her university days. The young people found a night spot where Russian youth hung out. Don and I spent our second and last night in Moscow over a simple meal in the Cosmos hotel restaurant. Was it time to mail the letters Marlow carried? Masha had already bought stamps and located envelopes for us. We wanted to get rid of them.

"It's too risky," Don argued. "Perhaps the envelopes could be traced back to us when they arrived in the central post office." He was convinced we should wait until the last night in the USSR when we would find a post box in Leningrad. He'd heard there had been a recent crackdown by the KGB on Americans trying to make contact with refuseniks.

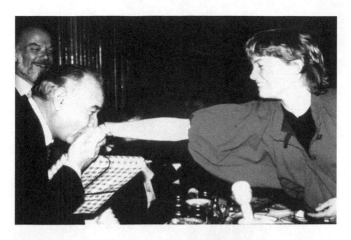

Vladimir and our bus took us to the airport for our flight to Tashkent the next day. On the plane, we began to relax. Uzbekistan was far from Moscow and the Kremlin's direct influence. The Uzbek mayor, Vahkid Kazimov, had reason to greet us warmly. Our cities had been paired through the sister-city program since 1973, quietly functioning under the radar of each of our nation's capitals despite escalating tensions between the heads of state.

Tashkent was a modern city, rebuilt in a massive effort by people from all over the USSR after its near total destruction in the earthquake of 1966. None of the stunningly beautiful ancient Arabic architecture remained. Happily, we would see the blue and gold mosaic covered mosques when we traveled to Samarkand a few days later. For now, we deplaned in a modern glass, concrete, and steel airport darkened by a moonless evening. A row of adorable five-year-olds gave color to the drab setting. Little Uzbek girls in red coats and enormous white bows sitting on top of their uniformly cut black-bobbed hair held daffodils out to us as we walked between their smiling faces. Swept forward with the other dignitaries, I felt like a star, wanted and adored. What a contrast to Moscow!

Our bus roared through Tashkent's nearly empty streets, led by uniformed police on motorcycles. Flashing red lights and shrill sirens announced our passage. We looked at each other in astonishment, unsure what to make of this reception. Were there no cars in Tashkent? Had everyone been cleared out? We were the first delegation between the two cities since Tashkent's Mayor Kazimov had traveled to Seattle to establish the Tashkent Peace Park on Capitol Hill in 1974. We guessed this was such a big event, they cleared away any late evening traffic for us.

The following day, the mayor and his committee had chosen to showcase key sites. We were taken to a primary school where I had to pull in the edges of my black linen suit jacket to avoid the freshly-painted desks and doorways, still wet and glistening in bright reds, yellows, and blues. Our next stop was a subway station, completely devoid of other riders, where our footsteps echoed on the stone. We went down the escalator and entered an empty train carriage smelling faintly of disinfectant. We murmured to each other that they must have cleared everyone away, perhaps to protect us or to shield us; we knew not which.

The subway ride spilled us out into a large market square filled with people. The open area was ringed by tables of melons—all colors and sizes—vegetables, bags of rice, wheat, corn, beans, chilies, more fruit, plastic combs, hair gadgets, pens, and tablets. Vats of sputtering cooking oil brimming with spices and garlic got me sneezing. People hawked their wares in melodious phrases punctuated by guttural consonants quite foreign to my ear. A child darted between our legs pursued by a shrill older sister. Orange, yellow, and red geometric designs in silk cloth of the traditional women's dresses filled the square. Dark eyes fringed in flowered shawls or simple head scarves stared at us.

Each of us carried our manila envelopes with our portion of the signed peace letters. We began approaching shopkeepers, children, passersby with copies of the letter. Tentatively, hesitating before our advance, we watched one person after another accept the offering and stand still to read the Russian words.

"Our two nations must work together to create peaceful means of resolving conflicts and take steps to reduce the danger of nuclear war."

One of us handed a letter to a group of construction workers taking a tea break. These men had the broad, round faces and high hairlines, the blue eyes and ruddy skin of Russians, not the dark Turkic appearance of the merchants. Several of the workers read over the shoulders of the one reading out loud; they looked at us, surprised to have strangers, foreigners handing out such a message. They approached us, hands reaching for more copies, big smiles on their faces, even a few tears. One boy on a bicycle sped away and came back moments later with three more boys, their mothers panting to catch up. All wanted letters. A young girl brought sweets to several people in our group, asking to exchange them for more copies.

I wandered to the edge of the crowd, reaching out to two women tending a stall with apricots, pears, ripe apples, quinces, peaches. They grinned as I handed them letters. Then their eyes widened as they looked over my shoulder. They pulled back, one woman's hand flying to her mouth as if to stifle a cry. Swirling around, I was face-to-face with a young police officer. He wagged his stick at me, took my elbow in one hand and reached for all my remaining letters, his billy club dangling from his wrist. I panicked, cursing myself for my habit of going off on my own. I looked frantically toward the group for help and saw Vladimir rushing to my rescue. A good six inches taller than the officer and twenty years his senior, Vladimir explained that the mayor had given us permission to hand out the letters. "Go!" whispered Vladimir. I rushed toward the others from our group leaving our guide to smooth things over with the police officer.

It was time to board our bus and attend the official sister-city event. My brush with the police sobered our group. Ruth took my arm as we walked into the dark-paneled hall leading to the offices of the mayor. She and I and the others were thrilled and a little surprised to see backlit, glass-fronted cabinets with pictures of Seattle's Mayor Ullman and Uzbekistan's Mayor Kazimov in the Peace Park on Capitol Hill far away in Seattle. Salish Indian carvings, engraved plaques, and memorabilia from that long ago face-to-face visit made me wonder just how heavily the firm hand of the Kremlin rested on this mayor and his Uzbek staff, some Russian, some Turkic.

Inside the meeting room, a long, open rectangle of tables held Uzbek dishes, white porcelain decorated with gold trim and cobalt blue medallions with gold-edged flowers. Plates overflowed with dried apricots, raisins, almonds, and peanuts, dates covered in sesame seeds, sugar coated balls of ground dried fruit and nuts. Pots of tea and small round bowls for drinking marked our places. We sat facing an equal number of Uzbek men and women, government officials and supporters of the sister-city relationship. Don, Virginia, and Masha sat at the head table with Mayor Kazimov and his deputies. Vladimir was on hand to translate.

The mayor began the formalities with a warm welcome speech. Marlow snapped pictures. Don stood to make his remarks of gratitude for our reception and to state the purpose of our trip. "We have come to ask you, the citizens of Tashkent, to join with us to encourage our governments to avoid nuclear war so that our children and our communities will thrive in mutual friendship for generations to come." He went on to explain the nature of the letter, that forty-two thousand of our citizens had signed it, and that it was our privilege to pass out copies to people in the Tashkent public market earlier in the day.

As I watched him speak, I noticed his open blue eyes and careful goatee, his lean face, average height, and slim waist. He was a dead ringer for Lenin. It was obvious, his face silhouetted against the proverbial portrait of the most favored leader plastered on the chamber's wall. I could see that others noticed the likeness, too.

After speaking, Don handed the mayor the unrolled poster with the copy of the letter in three languages. Days before our departure from Seattle someone had the idea of printing the poster not only in Russian and English, but in Uzbek, too. The mayor passed the poster on to his deputy and proceeded with the presentation of gifts.

Seconds later, the staffer, having read the poster and discovered the Uzbek translation, tugged at the mayor's sleeve, interrupting the proceedings. He pointed to the letter in Uzbek, Cyrillic script with slight differences. The mayor took the poster into both hands and shushed the crowd. Their ethnicity had been acknowledged. He began to read to the assembly in Uzbek. Smiles spread on every face. The Uzbeks looked at each other and stood to reach across the tables, grinning broadly, gold and steel teeth gleaming. They were thanking us for recognizing them, people living under the reach of the Soviet Union but not Russian. In Uzbekistan, all government people were required to work in the Russian language and many were ethnically Russian, transplanted to Uzbekistan for the top government jobs. It was not obvious to me who was Russian and who Uzbek but it was clear that addressing them as Turkic-speaking people acknowledged their Republic as different. They embraced our gesture wholeheartedly.

Virginia remembers the conversation she had with the deputy mayor that evening. "For years we've been waiting for you to come. I lost both of my sons and my husband in the war. I don't want to lose my grandchildren."

We awoke the next day to front-page, Russian-language newspaper reports of our marketplace letter distribution. The paper carried a picture of a young man straddling his bicycle, hands on the handlebars holding a letter, his bill cap tipped up above his intent, smiling face. Another picture showed the construction workers. A third picture under the front-page banner showed one from our group grinning broadly at three Uzbeks each receiving letters. We were a sensation, having done something against the law that did not bring retribution but applause.

The feeling of breakthrough peacemaking was not to last for long. When we arrived at Tashkent State University for an official tour, the mayor's deputy, a squarish woman standing about five foot two, cornered Virginia. The deputy wagged her finger under Virginia's nose chastising us for distributing the letter.

"You were not given permission to hand out the letter. You were to give them to us so we could do that." She insisted on taking the remaining manila packets of peace letters. She would take care of that distribution for us.

On our final day in Tashkent, the big event was a peace rally staged in a public square near Tashkent State University, ending with an evening dinner gala and an Uzbek traditional dance performance. Our group stepped from the bus into a waiting crowd of neighborhood folk and university students who we assumed had been dismissed from class to create a crowd. A platform with a dozen chairs already occupied by university and city officials, microphones, and a podium awaited Don and Virginia. The rest of our group dispersed among the locals. An intense blue sky set off the creamy yellow of the university building at our backs.

A long red banner reading "Peace" in Russian and another asking for an end to war in English hung from the flat roof where a dark-skinned man in a traditional Uzbek skull cap, a black *tubeteika*, and another in a typical Russian *ushanka* fur hat with ear flaps, leaned on their elbows watching the proceedings.

The university president opened the program with welcoming remarks and turned the microphone over to an old Soviet veteran in a uniform bristling with medals and ribbons. Don's face was passive, relaxed, but both his eyes scanned the crowd like an owl. As he listened to the official translator, I noticed a change in Don's demeanor. His jaw clenched and he narrowed his eyes in concentration. The old Russian's tone changed from the celebration of the mutual fight against the Germans to harsh clipped challenge. I watched Don fumble with the slim notebook he carried. He seemed to listen, but I could see he was working out how to handle this shift. He fingered his tie, studied his notes. I watched him take in a deep breath, let it out slowly. He squared his shoulders and waited for the Russian's speech to end. The final sentence from the war hero was loaded with accusation: Our president had called the USSR an evil empire. Would Mr. Bell care to comment on this insult?

President Reagan's March 8 address to the National Association of Evangelicals in Orlando, Florida, in which he condemned the USSR, declaring it had made "the aggressive impulses of an evil empire," had occurred three weeks earlier. The speaker's challenge was completely out of character with the peace rally in which we were engaged. Don and Virginia had already been challenged about Reagan's speech while we were in Moscow. It was not expected in our sister city.

Don stepped to the microphone. He chose his words carefully, taking in the faces in the crowd. He spoke slowly, pausing after each phrase to wait for the translation. "We come in peace. We are ordinary independent citizens, not sponsored by our government. Our leaders speak angry words. We speak kind, personal words to each other. We love our country as you love yours. We want to see our children grow up and marry, as do you. As people, we can know each other and wish for each other's happiness."

He went on to emphasize the will of ordinary men and women as more important, even more powerful than one leader's angry words. He paused. There was a staccato of applause around the square. My heart swelled with pride. The grace in his manner, his language, his sincerity burned deep, filling me with respect and admiration. Don continued, "People of Tashkent, join with us to work for peace, no matter what our government leaders say." The applause grew, heads nodded around the square.

Later, over drinks in our hotel, we all learned what had happened up there on that platform. Don had picked up on the shift in tone in the soldier's speech, guessing that he was going to have to answer to President Reagan's condemnation of the Soviet Union.

OUR SISTER-CITY DUTIES FINISHED, WE boarded a bus the next day for Samarkand with only one official event on our calendar. The four-hour ride gave ample opportunity for debriefing. We had delivered the peace letters to individual Uzbeks. We had danced, talked, eaten with every sort of person in Tashkent. We had firm commitments for future teaching exchanges between our two universities. We were ready to take in the breathtakingly beautiful ancient city.

Wandering through the narrow streets of Samarkand, song poured over us, coming from a young man who stood on an ancient wall entertaining no one in particular. The scent of spices heated in hot oil wafted from shops along the stone path. A couple of the boys in our group played Frisbee in the great square, central to the 2700-year-old city, former capital of Tamerlane and of Genghis Khan before him.

The blue-domed mosque gleamed in the brilliant sunlight. I was awestruck by the large stone arch of the Ulugh Beg Observatory, a place of staggering sophistication and mathematical genius. Ulugh

Beg was built in the fourteen hundreds as an astrological instrument, one of the first of its kind. Marco Polo, who had traveled the Silk Road would have passed from Venice to China through Samarkand in the thirteenth century. Multicolored tiles on the facade of the impressively preserved buildings delighted us with their geometric patterns.

We delivered one of our signed peace letters to a welcoming Imam at a beautiful mosque. Amim Hatib invited us in. We left our shoes at the doorway and accompanied him into a bright, sunlit social hall where we listened to him, with Vladimir translating, explain the peace message in the Koran. He signed the letter on behalf of his congregation. His profession of love warmed our group.

Two days in the ancient capital was too brief.

Arriving in Leningrad (Saint Petersburg) for the final two nights felt like a return to the West. We were at home in this European city built by Peter the Great and his wife Catherine with their Italian architects and French artistic sensibility. Ice still clogged the Neva River. People were bundled in fur and leather against the deep chill. But the sun shone on the graves of the half-million people who died during the 872-day siege by the Germans in World War II. Cut daffodils graced the stone markers. The air was soft and carried the pungent scent of thawing marsh grasses.

Our one full day flew past. We were hurried through the Hermitage art museum with no time to linger and absorb the modern masters' works collected by Russians. A tour bus whisked us past the great monuments and palaces.

Two women from our group and I escaped the official afternoon meeting requiring Don's and Virginia's attendance and visited Tikhvin Cemetery in the garden of Alexander Nevsky Monastery. Marlow had also ducked out of the meeting, tired of recording carefully orchestrated talk on film. Instead, he caught our joyous faces as we paid homage to several great musicians who had stayed in Russia, often suffering censorship and artistic control—Tchaikovsky, Rimsky Korsakov, Mussorgsky, and Borodin. I had played the flute in many of their orchestral compositions. The Soviet State continued to manipulate creative artists and scientists alike. Urgency surged through me to get those letters from Marlow's camera bag into mine and into the mail to the refusenik families before we left the next morning. We'd successfully smuggled the letters to the refuseniks all the way here and now it was time to mail them.

When we all met in our hotel for the final dinner, the room was full of talk about the adventures of the day. Ruth and her young travel partners had gone to the official meeting and taken part in the formal conversations. Ruth had become increasingly interested in the nuances of history and the current political scene. All five of them expected to report to their classes about our experiences.

The stamped letters were in the envelopes Masha had provided, tucked into Don's coat pocket.

We excused ourselves early and set off in the night, marine air blowing gently off the Gulf of Finland. The Pribaltiiskaya hotel was situated at the far west end of Vasilyevsky Island, a few hundred yards from the Baltic Sea. We interlocked elbows and strode inland to see Peter the Great's statue in Senate Square.

"It got the name Bronze Horseman from a poem by Pushkin," Don explained, remembering the young man who grinned when he checked our luggage, having noticed Don's volume of Pushkin's poetry. "It's such a popular place, there are sure to be people about. It's still early by European dining standards."

We left Pribaltiyskaya Square and walked toward the grounds of two old churches and the Smolenskoe cemetery, then skirted the parkland to Maly Avenue and the northern arm of the Neva River to the east. We talked of many things as we passed other couples and groups of people enjoying the spring thaw. Red coals of cigarettes and soft voices preceded people as they moved from the wide, dark sidewalk into pools of yellow lamplight along the way. Nothing seemed threatening in any way. We had told no one we were going, trusting this city, a threshold to Europe, to be safe. "I'll bet you didn't suspect people would notice your likeness to Lenin," I teased. "Or that you'd have to speak to Reagan's mean speech about the Russians."

"They tried to make us the villains. I just sidestepped it."

"Brilliantly, I might add."

"Hasn't Ruth become sophisticated! She asked me so many questions. She reminds me of you when you were her age."

"That makes you sound ancient. You pulled me into this sister-city business. Now, there's no stopping me. I can't wait to get home and put something together to take to DC. I want our senators and representatives to know what this has been like. Instead of five sister cities between us and the USSR, there should be dozens. I hope Marlow creates something fantastic with his pictures."

"Virginia and I and several of the others are already planning the next Target Seattle. We decided to call it Soviet Realities. There's a meeting next week."

"Work gets in the way, don't you think?"

We both laughed. Spotting the spires of Andreyevsky Cathedral, we turned toward the southern arm of the Neva, Saint Isaac's Cathedral, the Bronze Horseman, and most importantly, the central post office.

We crossed the Blagoveshchenskiy Bridge, and turned east along the Admiralty Embankment. Groups of people stood around the monument, laughing and smoking, wearing fur coats and hats, leather gloves, and scarves. We were overheated by our four-mile walk, but glad to have our winter coats on.

"Let's get this done and get back to the hotel." I urged us on to the central post office, just beyond the cathedral. A blue letterbox was affixed to the front wall labeled почта. Just as Don lifted the door and slipped the letters in, a police car made a slow turn into the intersection. I grabbed Don in a panic. He enveloped me and we kissed, leaning against the post office building wall. We staggered a bit, laughed nervously. The police car didn't pause, but sped up the street as if answering an emergency call. Our laughter, kisses, and hugs became genuine and we nearly collapsed with relief. The letters were gone, mailed to the two Jewish families.

Returning to the Bronze Horseman, we easily hailed a taxi and spent the few rubles we had left getting ourselves back to the hotel.

Packing my suitcase to return to Seattle that night, I felt immense relief. The letters, both secret and acknowledged, had been delivered. We'd forged deep connections with many people. The Russians and Uzbeks saw that we were free, free to leave the US, to pay our own way to visit their country, and to have opinions different from our government.

We spent the brief stopover in Helsinki in the international waiting area. During our wait, we gathered quietly and reverently in an impromptu Easter vigil. We offered prayers of gratitude and of hope that love would triumph over hatred. Once on the plane to Seattle, nearly everyone fell asleep, exhausted from the fast-paced, emotional ten days behind the Iron Curtain.

Seattle's anti-nuclear crowd stood three- to four-deep at our arrival gate on April 3, 1983, Easter Sunday. Television and radio crews captured the co-leaders' stories of handing out the peace letters. Parents, spouses, faith leaders, and Target Seattle committee members cheered our arrival with balloons and flowers for their peace emissaries.

HOME ON LAKE WASHINGTON BOULEVARD, the three of us lugged our suitcases to our rooms and changed into jeans. Don and I wandered into the garden—he to inspect the lettuces, germinated, along with the weeds, and I, clippers in hand, to see what was blooming. The damp air differed from Leningrad in temperature—warmer in Seattle—and in scent, no saltwater marsh here. The loamy soil, the yellow blossoms of mahonia, Oregon grape, and new sword fern shoots gave off the smell of a lake shore forest. A wind had brought down branches from the aging *Autumnalis*. It stretched to the top of the third-floor dormers but was not healthy. Its blossoms had decayed to rust giving the new leaves a dirty appearance. All the other ornamental and fruit-bearing trees announced Easter with pure brightness. The thought came, as it had come off and on since we'd taken ownership of this three-story brick Tudor eleven years earlier, "Just cut the thing down now and get something more ordinary started."

I found pussy willow and forsythia branches to brighten the fire place mantle. Ten days' worth of mail was piled on the hall table. Don and I stood culling the important pieces. Over glasses of sherry, we listened to the answering machine messages. Uncle Tom called to ask about the refusenik letters and the plans for the next Target Seattle. Ruth's teacher asked when she could tell her fellow students at the Northwest School about her experiences. We were weary and jet-lagged, but nothing could dampen our excitement for the next steps toward preventing nuclear war. In my impatience, I could think of little else.

MONDAY'S REENTRY WAS A SLOG in the Northwest drizzle—Ruth to school by bus, Don walking to the university, and me on my bicycle up through Interlaken park to the cathedral. I was full of dread. I didn't want to answer to a boss. Dean Tennis was back from his sabbatical. He announced a change in the staff organization that was not comfortable for me.

He made it clear that our administrative structure would conform to the formality peculiar to Episcopal cathedrals: every member of the program staff is called a canon. I stammered, "I think being called a canon would change my role. My effectiveness comes from being part of the congregation, sitting in the pew like everyone else. People talk to me without hesitation, as equals."

After an awkward pause, I added, "I hate titles of any kind. They separate people. It has been refreshing to call you by your first name, not Father Cabby. Maybe that's a little confusing to some, but not for me. That's been important to me. Cabby, I can't be a canon, even if it's only a title and nothing more."

"Think about it for a few days."

He concluded our meeting by handing me Ken Blanchard's little book, The One Minute Manager. Sick with turmoil, I grabbed my umbrella and went to Volunteer Park, reading as I walked. Dean Tennis had changed so much about the formal Episcopal hierarchy. He instituted the election of the senior warden, normally appointed by the priest as the lay leader of the governing board. He instructed us to call him by his first name, getting rid of titles. I had loved this job, and the collegial spirit of the staff, ordained and lay. But in the four years as I read the Gospel and worked out my own interpretation, I couldn't find my place alongside the ordained staff.

Don wasn't any help. He didn't understand or empathize with my study of the feminine face of God, the role of women in the church. My frequent complaints about work fell on indifferent ears. I found a group of lay women who worked in the church. We had been meeting weekly to read and discuss feminist theology. What I learned tore me away. Cabby doesn't remember giving me Ken Blanchard's book, but I do. It pushed me over the edge. I'm sure now that he was trying to help me organize my thoughts, continue a job he wanted me to do. In spite of his kind coaching, I could not work for the church anymore. Impulsively, I returned to the cathedral, knocked on Cabby's door and told him I would resign my position effective the following Friday.

In my mind, my leanings toward feminist theology and against the church justified my leaving. I felt a surge of self-satisfaction and I couldn't wait to get home to tell Don I was on to something else.

At dinner that night, I told Don what I had done. His jaw dropped.

"How can you do this to me?"

"What do you mean? I thought you'd be happy for me. I've complained about how hard it is to stand on my own two feet in staff meetings. I've felt like one priest or the other was always looking over my shoulder, changing what I've created. It's like being rescued all the time. What if I did make a mistake? I never get to see what happens when my projects don't work." Don and I both knew the title of canon was a flash point, a convenient reason to quit working in the church system.

"But the money. We need your income."

I couldn't meet his eyes, so much confusion scrambled my thinking. Thank goodness, Ruth was at a meeting and not at the table to hear this.

I'd always considered it a privilege to work, the small salary a gift, unearned and unimportant. We'd never talked about the value of my financial contribution. I was shocked to discover he counted on my little bit. Don's reaction scared me. Anger rose up in my throat. I'd lost the clear path to an academic future in Spanish when we moved from the University of Kansas to Seattle to further Don's career. After three unhappy years of no paid work at all, I'd found a secretarial job with a project at the university, which turned into an adjunct faculty position. I wanted independence, something of my own away from family obligations. I fell into paid work at the cathedral after volunteering to organize weekend seminars and weeknight classes. I was good at what I did and went from half time to three-quarter time and a bigger salary.

Don broke the tense silence.

"Ruth starts college in the fall. How are we going to pay for two girls in college at once? What happens if this acting dean position disappears. Then where would we be?"

Nearly in tears, I shrugged my shoulders and got up to clear the table. I had no excuse to offer. I hadn't put the numbers together, letting Don handle the big financial picture. Memories of his words in letters written during our courtship surfaced. I couldn't throw them at him now. He'd promised my father he'd be able to keep me in the comfortable lifestyle of my childhood, that I would not have to work, ever. I remembered reading those words at age eighteen and vowing I'd never be only a housewife and mother. I would never have held him to his romantic promises. But work for me had never been about the money, only the independence of purpose. We'd been a good team, frugal and conservative with our resources, partly in defiance of my father's predictions that poverty makes a difficult marriage. Don's anger was so confusing.

Ruth came through the door, ending the possibility of further discussion. We went to bed silent, in our own thoughts. I made up my mind to show him. I could make money by putting on workshops for women based on new research about feminine approaches to moral decision-making. My friend, a trained psychotherapist, created the courses which I would market. Not sure how much money I would be able to earn with these seminars, I pursued a couple of nonprofit executive director positions. Nothing inspired me. I wanted to tell our Tashkent story to as many people as would listen. That's all I had energy for. I had to get in touch with Marlow.

"How's it going? Have you got something we can use?"

"Betsy, you won't believe how this is coming together. Shelley and I have been working nonstop."

Shelley, Marlow's classmate and girlfriend, had let me in when I knocked on their apartment door one afternoon in the last week of April, a short three weeks since our return from Leningrad.

"And to think you didn't think it was worth photographing a bunch of tourists on a talking trip." I laughed at his infectious enthusiasm. The main room of their apartment was cramped and stuffy by design. Stale air was still. He wanted no breeze to disturb his creation as he sat on the swivel stool, legs spread, knees brushing the underside of the low light table. Slides lay on the surface. He had been completely absorbed, hunched over, moving pictures into position, arranging a double storyboard.

"We're creating a multimedia slide show with two projectors. A two-track cassette tape runs a dissolve unit and a receiver carries the sound to speakers." He gestured to the equipment he had borrowed from the photography lab at the university. I was fascinated by the technology and he explained the details to me.

"Can you borrow projectors, or raise the money—donations maybe—so we can take this on the road?" Marlow said.

"When do you need all the stuff?" I was sure it could be done.

"When do you want the show to be ready?"

"Don tells me the program for Target Seattle/Soviet Realities is coming together. The first event is October 29. Can you have it ready by then?"

"Absolutely." Marlow stood up, walked over to his wall calendar and lifted the pages. He marked a large X on the October date, then faced me, grabbed Shelley's hand for a big squeeze, and said the slide show would be ready.

It was Marlow who said he wanted to take this show on the road— inspire other towns to get a sister-city relationship going. Maybe even take the show to Washington, DC, I was all in. Why not?

The three of us bounced with enthusiasm.

"I'm heading to a church conference in DC next week," I said. "Why don't I go a day early and call on our elected delegates while I'm there? I can put together a packet to leave behind, a photocopy of the picture in the Tashkent newspaper when we were handing out the letters. A copy of the peace letter. And some points about the Jackson-Vanik Amendment to the trade agreement and getting rid of travel restrictions between the US and the USSR. Let them know we're putting together a slide show about the trip. It couldn't hurt."

They encouraged me. I wouldn't have a slide show yet, but I could start with a little door knocking at the offices of two senators and two congressmen.

A FEW DAYS LATER I was on a plane to Dulles airport to attend an Episcopal lay ministry workshop. Even though I wasn't working for the church any more, I was passionate about equipping people to put their faith into action and wanted to learn what I could. Don, skeptical about the lobbying effort, but too preoccupied with work and planning meetings to help strategize, was at least able to find a friend who lived in Virginia to put me up. On Friday, before the conference began, I could see all four of our elected officials.

It was an impulsive move with little preparation other than assembling four packets of leave-behind information. I called each office to let the staff know I was coming and hoped to see each elected official. Lobbying wasn't new to me. In previous efforts, I'd been part of statewide organizations mobilizing to change local laws. It never occurred to me to call any of the people Don and I knew who moved in political circles. I could have gotten some pointers as to how to get the most out of lobbying at the national level. Instead, I charged ahead, convinced that painting a verbal picture of people cooperating across political and social barriers would be enough. My enthusiasm would surely convince these men to do whatever it took to change the laws. Impossibly naïve, I now realize.

Don drove me to the airport. We stood for a minute on the sidewalk under the Departures sign. A quick kiss and squeeze of the hand, "You'll be fine," and he was gone.

Washington, DC, was in the throes of a spring heat wave. The air was thick and smelled of a mixture of trapped car exhaust and spent cherry blossoms. After parking my rental car, I walked to the senate office building and stood in front of the structure in a state of panic. I mouthed an opening sentence, then shook my head. I had no idea how to begin. Marlow's "Go for it!" pushed me. I did know why I had come. Inside, the click of my heels down the marble hallway gave a beat to the marching song playing in my head.

Senator Jackson was not available. He sent his hardline adviser in his stead. The woman, a few years my senior, listened to me stammer through my story, then dispatched me with the inflexible party line about peace through strength. I left my packet and walked back down the long hall. A flood of self-deprecating thoughts dampened my zeal for this lobbying business. The woman thought I was a naïve blue-sky idealist with no practical sense. Maybe she was right. Maybe we were all naïve to think citizens could make a difference. Was I a fool to think I could accomplish anything?

A thought flashed through my mind to find a pay phone and call Don. No. He hadn't dissuaded me from trying, but he didn't think my approach would get anywhere. I didn't want to admit defeat. Instead, I went back to the Mall and found a tree to sit under. What I knew in my heart was what we demonstrated with our visit to Tashkent. An exchange between people of different cultures was a model of the kind of program that, when involving many groups and many themes—cooking, soccer, park building, educator and physician exchanges, choir tours, and dance troops—could reduce the risk of first strike. In Seattle, hundreds of people were convinced of that fact.

Fortified, I got up and headed for Senator Slade Gorton's office. Gorton, too, was unavailable. He handed me off to a young aide who toed the same party line. The look of disbelief on his face and his remarks stayed with me. "They [the Russians] want what we have. There isn't enough to go around. We have to protect our resources from them."

ON MY WAY TO THE congressional offices, I walked across the great lawn in front of the Capitol Building and sat on the broad stone steps, gazing past the Washington Monument toward the Lincoln Memorial at the far end of the Mall. Several groups of school children flocked up the steps, teachers and chaperones keeping a watchful eye. Tourists in national dress posed for pictures; flash cameras created little electrical fireflies. Men in dark suits carrying attaché folders bent their heads together in earnest talk, taking the steps as though late for an important meeting. The grandeur of the setting put me in a state of wonder. How lucky to be born American, to have a voice and the right to speak in the halls of power. But would it make any difference?

Republican representative Joel Pritchard could see me. He had to win reelection every two years, so it was to be expected, but his opinion lined up with the administration. He invited me to call on him if I came back to DC.

I knew Mike Lowry. He spoke at Target Seattle. His fund raisers in Kay Bullitt's backyard were boisterous gatherings of Democrats.

"Betsy Bell, Aldon Bell's wife. Come on in."

His entire staff were seated around a polished oval table waiting to hear what I had to say. The sweat on my back evaporated; my breathing slowed down. An unhurried spaciousness filled the room. These were my people, full of hope for a different approach toward our adversaries in the Kremlin. They listened with complete attention as I described the camaraderie our group of travelers had enjoyed with the people of Tashkent. I explained that I'd come to lobby for direct flights between the US and the USSR and government support for cultural and educational exchanges. Our goal was to get rid of travel restrictions tied to trade and human rights violations and to inspire other US cities to pair up with cities in the USSR.

I was surprised when applause broke out. Several around that table had signed our friendship letter. They thanked me for taking it on their behalf.

A few staff members asked questions about the kinds of cultural exchanges we had in mind. "There is a Seattle restauranteur who is organizing an exchange of chefs from Tashkent who may come and cook a traditional Uzbek banquet in Seattle. Seattle schoolchildren are making ceramic tiles that will be used in the new Seattle Peace Park once a location is found. These are a couple of the many ideas that are bubbling up. Our trip photographer is creating a multimedia slide show about our experience. We're planning to bring it to Washington later this year."

Lowry ended the meeting summarizing the key points. Overturning the Jackson-Vanik Amendment would be difficult as long as the Soviets used the refuseniks as pawns in the trade battles. Cultural exchanges would be easier. He offered staff support if we needed it and encouraged me to bring the slide show. "I'll sponsor it and get the invitations out. Just let me know when."

As I shook hands all around the table and made my way outdoors, it was all I could do to stifle tears of gratitude. I needed Marlow's pictures. And the equipment to present them.

Back in Seattle, my time was tied up volunteering on several projects and organizing the next workshop my colleague would present for women participants. Finally, in mid-June, I visited Marlow's apartment. He sat on the same stool in front of the same light table, slides now in orderly groupings. He'd loaded several trays into the projectors, in front of which stood a microphone.

He turned to face me. "I'm working on the hardest part, the voice-over. Royer's interview from KING TV before our trip is perfect. He talks about us working together to make a great city, behind shots of an eight-man shell on Lake Union."

Charles Royer was Seattle's Mayor in 1983. His wife Rosanne was the chair of the Seattle-Tashkent Sister City Committee and had helped pave the way for our trip to Tashkent.

"Sara narrated a segment about Red Square. There's a speech of Don's at the mayoral reception, a couple of comments from some of the others I recorded on the trip. I'm trying to do the rest. But, Betsy, I have to stand up and do jumping jacks to get enough energy in my voice."

Marlow paused then and stared at the far wall.

I followed his gaze as he looked across the light table to the posters over his unmade bed. The beautiful scenes were from *National Geographic*, probably taken by his father. On a bedside table stood a photo of his younger self holding a camera focused somewhere in the distance. In the picture, his father stood next to him, pointing with one hand while the other guided his son's aim by lifting the camera. Marlow drew a deep breath, turned back to me and said he'd been to the doctor about a terrible pain in his left thigh.

"The doctors don't know what it is. Some rare thing. I've been through all kinds of tests. My dad visited. He wants me to go back to Washington, DC, to see specialists."

I wanted him to keep going with the slide show. I wanted him to stop everything and take care of this ominous pain. Were long hours in a semi-squat in front of his light table somehow related to the pain? How was I contributing to his fierce dedication to this project?

THE SUMMER WAS A BLUR. I filled two women's workshops and finished six months of Spanish tutoring for high school kids going to Central America with the *Amigos de las Americas para medical* volunteer program. After her graduation, Ruth traveled with a team to dig latrines in a remote village in Mexico. The house filled up with students—ours and the daughters of friends who lived elsewhere—home from college, looking for work. When Don wasn't at his office or teaching, he sat at his desk at one end of our bedroom, making phone calls, lining up speakers for Target Seattle/Soviet Realities.

Doctors ran Marlow through more tests that summer. Finally, weeks later, the diagnosis came. Marlow had a rare form of soft tissue cancer. When I told Don, he set his elbows on the desk and cradled his forehead in his hands. I was devastated.

AT THE END OF THE summer, on September 1, 1983, a Soviet jet fighter shot down South Korean airliner flight 007, killing 269 people on board, including a US congressman. The downed airline was one of the most critical events in the Cold War. The Boeing 747 strayed off course into Soviet airspace, an act some now consider espionage on the part of the West. At a press conference in Seattle, Senator Jackson bitterly denounced the Soviet Union for attacking the Korean airliner. Hours after the press conference, Jackson died of a massive heart attack.

Days later, Don came home from the university and announced he would try for Jackson's senate seat. I panicked at the thought of becoming the wife of a politician. Don would once again make a career move that would thwart any chance I had to build a career for myself. Ruth had just left for college. Our empty nest was my chance.

"Can we take a walk and talk about this?" I needed time. It had been a dream of Don's to serve in public office. While in the army before we married, he wrote long letters about the many national and international events of the Cold War, Adlai Stephenson's campaign for president in 1956, and various actions of senators and members of congress and what he would do if he were in their position. I wasn't surprised he thought of running for Jackson's seat. But I wanted nothing to do with life in Washington, DC.

Don and I walked side by side to the arboretum, just down Lake Washington Boulevard from our house. The park was bathed in the late afternoon sun that so often peeks out from under the daylong cloud cover. We walked in silence down Azalea Way, ignoring the muddy squish. Soggy drifts of big maple leaves strewn the way. An owl's call interrupted the silence.

"Have you asked anyone's opinion about running?" I said.

To my surprise and dismay, he'd gathered a small group of influential Democrats and asked them to test the possibility of support and money from the larger community. He was awaiting their replies.

"What do you think, Bets?"

I stopped walking and turned to face Don. "I don't know if I can support you in this. I just don't think I can. I'm afraid I would disappear completely."

We headed back toward our street, elbows locked, in silence. As our house came into view, I said, "The girls are gone. It's my turn."

Don said nothing for a long time. He loosened his hold and unlocked our elbows. My steps pressed leaves into the concrete under our feet. I was no longer the helpmate he'd groomed.

"What about your teaching career and the deanship?"

"They're less important to me than politics. Look what we've accomplished. How many people are coming forward to end the nuclear madness! With Jackson gone, we can increase the focus on diplomacy, less saber rattling."

"Don, I'm afraid running for office would destroy our marriage."

As we entered the back door to the kitchen, he said he would wait for the opinion of his advisers before making a final decision. I filled the silence with chatter about next weekend's women's seminar. I got him talking about the roster of speakers who'd said yes to Target Seattle. I reminded him I planned to go back to Bryn Mawr for an alumnae board meeting and had called Uncle Tom to see if he would come out for the opening Target Seattle event on October 29.

Night finally came. We walked upstairs and brushed our teeth. I pulled down the bedspread and clicked on the lamp on my nightstand. As Don climbed in between the sheets, he pleaded, "Don't give up on the idea quite yet."

Don told me days later that his mentors had urged him to continue with the public service leadership of Target Seattle and let political office go. I nodded, then wrapped my arms around his solid torso and pressed my head to his chest.

THE SLIDE SHOW—*PEOPLE TO PEOPLE, City to City*—was finished just after Labor Day despite Marlow's doctors' appointments and his fatigue. After much consultation, the University of Washington oncologists determined a course of treatment. Marlow would begin chemotherapy right after the Christmas holidays.

Marlow was eager to share his work. Saint Mark's was the perfect venue. News of Marlow's diagnosis swept through the committee and their friends. Even though the middle of September was frenetic with event planning and everyone's usual professional obligations, a big crowd showed up to see what he had created.

The lights in the cathedral's social hall dimmed and we focused on Marlow's stunning images of people attentive at meetings, examining newsprint on walls, discussing nuclear war, and coming up with ideas for how to influence our government. A mix of voices and music sped up or slowed down to convey the mood and support the story. Zhukov and the Soviet Peace Committee; the young Uzbek singer; the clash and tinkle of the great Uzbek tambourines; the dancing, feasting, and speeches in Tashkent; our translator Vladimir interpreting the mayor, the Imam, the decorated soldier; and our own voices in public speeches and in private conversations were all on screen. The show ended with the song "I Am One; You Are One" and beautiful faces flashed, one American, another Russian, another Uzbek until none of us were sure of the nationality and we knew nationality didn't matter. We were all one. When the lights came up, people dabbed at their noses. All stood to applaud. Marlow and his father walked to the front of the room. It was impossible to believe this handsome young man with a full head of hair, a broad grin, and sparkling eyes had cancer growing inside him.

"I'm going to beat this cancer," he told the audience while his father stood beside him. "I am going to beat this."

We all hoped and prayed he was right.

Marlow, Shelley, Virginia, Don, Marlow's dad, and others gathered at the refreshments table after the show. Marlow challenged all of us. "Take this to Washington. Take it all over the state. Get on the road."

"How about you taking it?" I suggested.

"Too many doctors' appointments. And chemo. Shelley can go for me."

Shelley said she could go during spring break in mid-April.

BY THE END OF SEPTEMBER, the ten-day Target Seattle/Soviet Realities program was set. The program opened and closed with events televised by KING-TV5. Virginia McDermott's committee organized in-home meetings where people all over the Puget Sound area could watch the programs on TV and call in responses to questions raised. Hundreds of meetings were planned. Marlow and Shelley would open the program with the slide show.

We were hoping Caspar Weinberger, Secretary of Defense would be one of the speakers.

Around that time, just before the academic year began, Don and I attended a team-building dinner party at President Gerberding's home.

University deans and their spouses were invited. Gerberding was still new to the UW presidency. He was quoted as saying our country was in a "period of confusion, uncertainty, plagued by a certain amount of cynicism and a good deal of pessimism and gloom." Hope was the antidote, the deterrent to the pessimism and doom that fueled the arms race. I determined to get him to a Target Seattle event—this dinner was my chance to approach him. I had tucked a couple of tickets to the opening event in my purse. During cocktails, I walked up to Gerberding and offered the tickets to him. He looked at me as if for the first time, and hesitated. A hush fell over the stately living room. Late afternoon sun filtered through the sheer curtains. An awkward freeze-frame of men and women with tipped stemware to their lips waited to return to business as usual. Finally, the president said, "I don't think my wife and I will be attending." He turned away from me and back to his conversation. My face flushed. I stepped back, returned the tickets to my purse, and looked for Don. He scowled at me from across the room. I spent the rest of the evening avoiding conversation and notice.

When we returned home, I waited for Don's reprimand. Nothing. Silence and busyness. That was all. It didn't occur to me then that there could be even greater consequences.

A month later, Uncle Tom and I sat in the front row as Don chaired the opening Target Seattle event by introducing the *People to People* slide show. When the final image faded to black and the lights turned back up, the audience whooped and applauded. My uncle looked at me, nodded, and patted my arm. I beamed.

The opening program was televised. Virginia and her team recruited hosts for 500 venues—living rooms, churches, and other public meeting spaces—to watch a panel discussion about the various ways to prevent nuclear war. The Reagan administration had tentatively agreed to send Casper Weinberger, Secretary of Defense, to present the government's policy, but instead sent Edward Rowney, retired general and Chief Arms Negotiator for the START treaty. Rowney, who restated the government's peace-through-strength position, spoke on a panel with others who represented different views. All week long, teach-ins brought hundreds of people out. Then, the final Sunday evening, the televised "Town Meeting" discussions took place again. Every participant played a part. Preventing nuclear war was everybody's business.

Edward Rowney didn't think nuclear war was anybody's business but the government's. In his talk, he said that the only person he knew who agreed with disarmament was his mother. That week, Hyde and Cabby Tennis gave a dinner party for about a dozen people in his honor. Rowney found himself in a room full of people who agreed with his mother. Virginia didn't get there in time for drinks, but later understood that some of what Rowney had said angered people. In spite of the delicious meal showcasing a large, stuffed zucchini from the Tennis' productive vegetable garden, the mood was awkward. During the meal, Rowney chatted with Virginia. She vividly remembers the conversation, ranging from friendly talk about children and how much coffee he'd needed to stay awake. At one point he said to her,

"The reason I agreed to come here was to find out what you people are thinking."

She told him she appreciated that. After a pause, he asked expansively, "What shall I tell the President when I return to Washington?"

"Tell the President that there are thousands of people here who are enraged by the threat of nuclear war."

The General literally jumped in his chair and responded, "I couldn't possibly tell the President that!"

"Why not?" Virginia remembers asking.

"Look, you don't have to worry about that. I am working very hard on all this. I will save you!"

"What if I don't believe you?"

"Then you aren't worth saving."

That comment was so outrageous—as much to Rowney as to Virginia—that they both just laughed.

SPRING ARRIVED—IT WAS TIME TO get the show to the East Coast. When I called Congressmen Lowry's and Pritchard's offices, they scheduled a showing in the rotunda of the Capitol Building. The US House of Representatives had conducted a bipartisan seminar called "Soviet Realities: Problems in the Pursuit of Peace," so they were primed for our message.

Don suggested calling others for showings. The idea resonated with people who had seen news clips of the huge numbers of people involved in Target Seattle events. We approached the coordinating office for all nongovernmental organizations (NGOs) and the United Nations, the various YMCAs in New York City, the Episcopal General Theological Seminary where my former colleague from Saint Mark's was back in school, Philadelphia's committee to establish a sister-city relationship with Leningrad, my alma mater, Bryn Mawr College outside Philadelphia, and the National Institute for Public Policy in Virginia. After Shelley and I confirmed venues, we booked our flights to New York.

Marlow drove Shelley and me to the airport. His cancer treatment had started some weeks earlier and his luxurious head of hair was gone. He helped us push our suitcases full of equipment to the United check-in and walked us to the Jetway in the north terminal.

"We'll check in with your dad at the National Geographic office in DC," I said as we waited to board the plane.

He kissed Shelley goodbye and gave me a hug, then walked back to the entrance. Once in our seats, Shelley and I looked at each other.

"Can you believe this?" I asked.

"Let's hope we don't mess up the slide trays or hookups or anything," she said.

"We just need to allow plenty of time. Each place will be different."

On the long flight, I worried again that I had pushed Marlow too hard. But Shelley reassured me Marlow had loved this work as she did. Shelley was an accomplished photographer herself and some of the slides in the show were from her portfolio. She'd been to many of the organizing meetings and would have gone to Tashkent with us if the cost hadn't been prohibitive. Shelley and Marlow's complete commitment to each other and their shared work struck me. My relationship with Don in all this work was much more push and pull.

After we landed in New York City, we went straight to the seminary. We had anticipated big audiences because of the national press coverage of September's massive turnout for Target Seattle/Soviet Realities. But we would discover the audiences would be smaller than hoped. People wouldn't flock to the slide show presentations, even when they were troubled by the threat of nuclear war and wanted to do something to prevent it.

We ate a quick bite, then set up the show for a smallish group of students and faculty. The next morning, we slept in, showered in a rush, then grabbed coffee and Danish on the way to the Sloan Street YMCA. We arrived around ten thirty, with plenty of time to set up the equipment. Our audience—unsuspecting regulars at the Y, ready to take in any program they put on—was smaller than I hoped. None of my friends managed to get there by crosstown bus, or walking, or subway, or whatever other means. They may have been terrified of imminent first strike, but couldn't manage getting to a show about a bold move on the part of a few ordinary citizens from Seattle.

Nevertheless, setting up the show was good practice. None of the technological challenges threw us off. Once back on the street with our suitcases strapped on the collapsible wheels, Shelley and I looked at each other.

"It's only one thirty. Why not go to the UN?" I said.

"Our contact there told us she didn't have time for us."

"What can it hurt?"

"OK." Shelley stepped off the curb to hail a cab. Two slowed down and then sped away, shaking their heads at the pile of suitcases. A third slowed down, asked where we were going and threw everything in his trunk. We sped east along thirty-fourth street to the East River, then up ten blocks to the United Nations complex. The green-glassed iconic tower of the Secretariat nearly blinded us as we stepped into the brilliant afternoon sun. Shelley and I gawked, mouths open, arms hanging at our sides, at the marble sweep of the General Assembly building. The huge member-nations' flags thunder clapped in the wind blowing off the river.

"Here goes nothing!" I said.

We walked up to the main visitor entrance, gave the security guard our contact's name and listened.

"They say they are from Seattle. Something about a slide show . . . no, they don't have an appointment, that's right. . . .. Let them in? OK. If you say so."

We couldn't believe it. Pushing the cases up to the great glass doors, we waited for what seemed like forever, wondering what would happen. Then there she was, Mrs. Shelley, holding the door open for us.

"Betsy and Shelley, is it? That's confusing. My last name is Shelley. There's no stopping you two strong Western women, is there?" She studied our linen suits, stockings, low heeled pumps, and the three cases we lugged behind us. "I had a cancellation. Come in and show me what you've got."

She led us to a small auditorium, then called an audiovisual technician. She invited Oleg Troyanovsky, permanent representative from the USSR to the UN, and one other staffer into the room. The three of them sat front and center. The lights went down. Thirty minutes later when the lights came up, Oleg began to speak. His voice caught. He pulled out his handkerchief, blew his nose, and tried again. Dabbing at his eyes, he said he wished his colleagues could have seen this. "Your group from Seattle—you did a brave thing." His companion nodded and looked down at his hands, snuffling noisily.

"I'm glad you came." Mrs. Shelley's voice wavered. "I'm especially glad I was available." She got up to walk us out. Before we left, the three of them took our hands in theirs.

"Thank you, thank you," Oleg said. "I just wish I'd been able to get more people in here to witness this. You people in Seattle have done something wonderful. I work with many groups trying to do what you have accomplished. Thank you again."

Back outside, we danced our load to the street. Only three people. It didn't matter. Who knew what ripple effect the presentation could have. Looking back, the adventure at the UN seems foolish, unorganized, with no big audience and no follow-up. Perhaps it was a wasted effort. Now I wish we had been better prepared. Naïve or not, some may have been influenced and some contribution made to the collapse of the USSR, already coming unraveled by economic and political unsustainability and corruption.

Shelley and I parted ways for the night. She had friends in New York who'd invited her to stay. My host at the seminary begged me to set up a private *People to People* showing. She'd missed the campus-wide event the previous night. Eager for any opportunity, I unpacked the suitcases. Without Shelley to help me, I didn't remember every step of the complicated setup. Fumble-fingered, I couldn't calm down enough to troubleshoot the problem and ended up manually projecting the slides side by side on their dining room wall and narrating the show without music, voices, or blending effects provided by the dissolve unit. When I turned up the lights, my former colleague, a priest, said,

"This is what you're showing to the senators?" I hung my head. My host reassured me that I'd done a good job and the show was fine. Her kind words didn't help.

The next morning, Shelley and I met at Penn Station and boarded Amtrak for Washington, DC, I had packed badly the night before, my brain still clouded by the shame of not being able to run the slideshow, and I ended up stuffing a few things into a grocery bag. When we arrived at Penn Station, the bags on collapsible wheels that Shelley pulled clattered to the platform and fell apart. I followed Shelley with our personal bags. We finally boarded the train with all of the luggage. I looked out the window as the train pulled away, and spotted the brown paper bag still on a seat at the station. I screamed, "My cosmetic bag. It's in that grocery sack." The string of pearls Don gave me on our wedding day was in that bag. An unmanageable sense of betrayal threatened to send me to my knees right there in the aisle. I didn't know how I would defend myself when he found out. Too often I'd been scolded for losing things. I clenched my jaw, shrugged, and said, "Forget it. Washington, DC, next stop."

Thirty chairs, a screen, and a projection table awaited us, dwarfed in one quadrant of the rotunda of the Capitol Building. Shelley and I set the show up without a glitch just as Congressmen Pritchard and Lowry and about twenty congressional aides, notepads in hand, arrived. As they took their chairs, other members of congress walked by, some pausing to watch briefly. The gazing eyes of Lincoln, Hamilton, Jefferson, and Washington looked down from the dome. John Trumbull's painting of the signing of the Declaration of Independence was overhead. The young aides seemed distracted, tapping pens on notepads, glancing around, as though they were overwhelmed by their function in the machinery of democracy. We—ordinary citizens—were in their midst to bring news and opinion from outside the Beltway. One more citizen effort to influence their bosses.

The show began, and the aides' faces never left the screen. One way I could tell if people were really paying attention was gauging their reaction to the slide of Don standing to speak at the mayor of Tashkent's reception. Sure enough, attendees chuckled and whispered of Don's resemblance to Lenin, whose full-sized portrait hung right behind him—they were tracking. Heads nodded to the rhythm of the

Uzbek dancers and drummers. A relaxation came over the group when the pictures of Leningrad melted into one another and the soundtrack slowed. The spring thaw in Marlow's images warmed those jaded, would-be politicians.

When the presentation was over, eyes stared off into the sweeping arches of the dome. In that brief silence, I hoped we might have broken through the cynicism. But the questions that followed challenged us.

"What good is this, really?"

"How can this type of connection change the political stance of the Soviet government? Or of ours?"

"How do you think cultural exchanges can slow down the threat of nuclear holocaust?"

"Given the instability of the government in the USSR right now, how can this person-to-person effort make any difference?"

It was true that Andropov had stepped down after only eight months as head of state in the Kremlin. The next man in line lasted three months. Chernenko had just come into power the day before our arrival in Washington. Tensions were greater than ever. Gorbachev wasn't to come to power until several years later, in 1988, and with him, perestroika reform and the openness of glasnost. How did we know our trip and the slides showing the upwelling of hope and action from Seattle could change anything? A few of the aides thanked us as they left. I believed those images would stay with them.

Our next stops were Fairfax County, Virginia, at the National Institute for Public Policy, followed by a train ride north to Bryn Mawr College, my alma mater, both of which provided welcoming audiences and enthusiastic applause for the show. But our most energetic audience by far was the Committee for Sister City Relations in Philadelphia, where they were trying to establish a pairing with Leningrad. We presented at the Friends Center in Center City, and attendees there pummeled us with questions afterwards. Their committee's agenda included helping the refuseniks leave Russia, which had led to protests by local interest groups. Jewish organizations felt establishing a sister city with Leningrad was a capitulation to the Soviets who treated Jews badly. After the show, several faces registered recognition of the lack of a political agenda in our trip and the emphasis on people meeting and knowing each other across international barriers. It wasn't until 1992 that Philadelphia managed to establish a sister-city relationship with Nizhny Novgorod, known as Gorky during the Cold War. The effort to establish ties with Leningrad never materialized.

When Shelley and I disembarked at Sea-Tac Airport, our men waited for us at the Jetway.

"I can't believe you did this." Don grinned. He'd taken the lost pearls in stride. "A few mishaps, but a real triumph."

Marlow hugged Shelley, then me. "Lots of people have called asking when you can take the show to their place," he said.

"A big meeting of Ploughshares next week wants the show for the main presentation," Don said. "They've booked the auditorium in Denny Hall. And I'm teaching a class at Saint Mark's the first week in May with the show as the centerpiece."

A group of Russian religious leaders coming in May would be the first foreign visitors to experience Marlow's beautiful message of cooperation. Over the next months, in a dog-eared blue folder, we logged sixty-five *People to People* showings to twenty-five hundred attendees. From the first entry at the Episcopal Seminary in New York City April 9, 1984, to February 25, 1986, each presenter wrote his or her name, the location, and how many saw the show. Don, Shelley, Marlow, Virginia, and two others from the trip, Carmen and Jean, plus one of the Target Seattle student volunteers, Don's right-hand man, Peter Holt, and I all lugged the bulky suitcases, set up the equipment, and dimmed the lights. The show traveled as far as Denver, Colorado; Notre Dame, Indiana; and my hometown, Muskogee, Oklahoma. We covered Washington State from Omak, Leavenworth, Cashmere, Roslyn, Yakima, Chelan, and Wenatchee to the east; beyond to Boise, Idaho; up and down the I-5 corridor from Bellingham to Federal Way, Tacoma, Olympia and on to Portland.

The committee heard so much interest in engaging local people in towns across the state that they decided to host one more event: Target Washington co-chaired by Congressman Foley and US Senator Dan Evans (who was appointed to Jackson's seat and then elected to the position). The Seattle-based conference in mid-April 1984 continued the following October with a one-day public event in each of three cities: Spokane, Yakima, and Vancouver. Don was very involved in all the planning for these events, taking more time from his university job. He and Shelley presented the slide show several times east of the mountains.

After the October conferences, the steering committee discussed their future purpose, took stock of three Target Seattle events designed to educate and mobilize that occurred from 1982 to 1984 and the plethora of new organizations forming to continue peace-building through cultural exchanges. They decided to disband. The mission was accomplished—hundreds of people were involved in creating a future without nuclear war, a future of friendships across the continents.

By the end of the 1980s, dozens of cities across the United States would line up to request sister cities in the USSR. They saw Seattle as a model primarily because our connection with Tashkent never wavered in spite of the invasion of Afghanistan by the USSR, the Korean airliner incident, and local pressure by Russian and Baltic Americans to exit the relationship. Not all of the cities who wanted to connect with USSR cities succeeded. As Rosanne Royer (longtime chair of the Seattle-Tashkent Sister City Committee) pointed out, "The fact that the first US/USSR Sister Cities International gatherings chose to hold their meetings in Tashkent and Seattle is a testimony to Seattle's influence." Many newly-organized Seattle groups—the Peace Chorus, the Peace Park builders, amputee soccer players, to name a few—traveled to or were planning trips to the USSR. Citizen diplomacy involving hundreds of people was taking off from both sides of the Iron Curtain. The warlike rhetoric coming from the Kremlin and the White House softened. By 1988 Gorbachev was in power. He and Reagan communicated in the conciliatory terms of glasnost. When asked about his evil empire speech in March of 1983, Reagan said, "That was then. This is now." Many Soviet Jews who had waited years were suddenly released to take up residence in Israel. I often wondered about the two families of refuseniks and whether they received our letters.

The end of the program was a time of transition for all of us. Don would be less busy with no Target Seattle to chair, though he would continue working with Russian visitors. Shelley traveled all over the state presenting the slideshow during the fall and into the winter months, while Marlow's cancer treatments shifted from curative to experimental therapies. Marlow wore caps friends knit for him, and looked thinner and more exhausted every time we saw him. Our daughter Priscilla called from Florida announcing that she wanted to go to college. Grace finished up her ordinary seaman job with NOAA, decided to go back to school, too, and roomed with Priscilla at the Evergreen State College in Olympia. We now had all four daughters in college at once. My feminist workshops weren't making any money. Long runs in the arboretum became my escape.

I've got to find a job.

Why can't Don and I talk about this?

It's all Target Seattle and the Russians for him.

THANKSGIVING 1984 CHANGED EVERYTHING.

On the Wednesday before Thanksgiving, Don walked as usual to his office of Acting Dean of Continuing Education. He opened the door and saw a pink slip on his desk. The note instructed him to remove all personal belongings immediately. He was no longer needed as dean, acting or otherwise.

Don trudged home in the late afternoon gloom, and found me in the kitchen putting away groceries for the family feast the next day. In a thin voice, he said he'd been fired. He needed the car to drive back to the university to collect his things. Before I could ask anything, he disappeared down the basement steps to find a box. He brushed past me, grabbed the car keys from their hook and opened the door to the garage.

"Wait!" I called after him. "Do you want help?"

He slumped his shoulders, shook his head, and was gone.

I leaned against the counter and raised my hands to my face, memories of Don's father's humiliation in his late fifties flooding my thoughts. Don's father managed his hometown equity exchange back in the Texas panhandle and had made what he judged an aggressive but safe investment in commodities futures with the farm co-op's surplus funds, but the profit didn't materialize. His father, Don's grandfather, who was chairman of the equity exchange board, called an emergency meeting. Don's father was fired. Two years later, he died from brain cancer.

Like his father, Don never voiced dark thoughts. He would, I knew, return to full-time teaching. We jokingly called it "back to the bench," the real work of an academic. He'd accepted his original post as dean at the university in 1969 on the condition of tenure in History. Sure enough, money dried up for innovation in undergraduate education—the focus of his first deanship—in the late seventies. He taught full time only a few years before he was tapped for the second administrative post. This time was different—he was fired, not let go because of budgetary changes. I worried he wouldn't weather the shame—that he'd turn inward like his dad.

The Thanksgiving break sped by. Grace and Priscilla joined us from Evergreen. Don and I took long, wet runs in the arboretum, but there was no talk of his sudden change in status. On Monday, when Don called to ask why he was being dismissed, the provost said, "You have other interests."

Had I crossed the line Don carefully maintained between his political and university lives when I invited President Gerberding to attend the Target Seattle event? Was I somehow to blame?

Don kept quiet about getting fired and made no further attempt to discover the cause. With an air of silent resignation, he added a couple of courses to his teaching load, one on the history of Canada and another on Southern Africa, both in his areas of expertise as an Oxford-trained British Empire scholar.

Around the first of December, I carried a lunch bag into the basement of Miller Hall on the university campus, in search of Don's new office, hoping to talk. I finally located his nameplate in the farthest corner of the darkest corridor of the building. When I cracked open his office door, I stood face-to-face with the end of a freestanding floor-to-ceiling bookcase crammed with tomes. The space between the center bookshelves and the floor-to-ceiling shelves on each wall was so narrow, I had to pull the bag in front of my body to squeeze through. An old desk and two straight-backed gunmetal gray chairs at the far end were the only furnishings. Don rose to give me a kiss, took my bag, and set it down next to the industrial-issue wastebasket. I sat in the chair next to his desk. The one barred window, its glass embedded with protective wire, gave so little midday light, he needed the desk lamp on. The lamp's chain hung over a black desktop organizer with pens, pencils, chalk, paper clips, a pair of scissors, and bits of cut-up paper for note taking. A large atlas on a stand opposite the window against the inside wall was open to Rhodesia, not yet updated to Zimbabwe to reflect its independence from Great Britain in 1980. He moved a yellow pad to make room for the sandwiches and quartered tomatoes I laid out.

Feigning cheerfulness, I said, "How do you like your new space?"

"See for yourself. It is a hellhole, the worst faculty office in the entire History Department. I can see only one student at a time. I've been demoted horribly."

"Pretty bad," I agreed. "Maybe a plant would help? Or a floor lamp?"

He shrugged, then picked up his sandwich and took a bite.

"Talk to me, Don. Don't be like your father."

"I don't want to bother you with my problems."

"Then talk to someone else. A therapist." I wanted to ask if I had made everything worse by going off on my own so much, but didn't know how to begin. I set the sandwich down half-eaten. We finished lunch in silence.

On the walk home, I vowed to follow up on a friend's lead for a sales job right after the first of the year. Ten days later, all four daughters came home from college to celebrate Christmas. I was in no mood for putting on a show of abundance when everything felt pinched and scarce.

"I resign. I'm not doing Christmas!" I announced at breakfast on the twenty-fourth.

"We'll do it," the girls chorused, then rummaged through the cupboards for cookie makings. Pretty soon there was a list. Don, surrounded by his daughters, headed out to the car to shop. As they waved goodbye, someone said, "We'll go to the cabin."

We shared use of a small cabin on French Creek. It would be ours for Christmas. In a few hours, the car was packed and we were off. A light dusting of snow covered the ground when the high beams pulled through the gate. After unloading, Don and Eleanor and Ruth took flashlights and went off into the forest to cut down a tree. Grace pulled out ornaments she'd bought on a trip with my parents during her years off from college. Priscilla had picked up a string of lights.

"We need music," someone said. I walked out to the car for a tape of carols I'd been playing and popped the cassette into the boom box. I couldn't stay mad with a roaring fire, mulled wine, Christmas music, a decorated tree, and a feast of popcorn, cheese, and Granny Smith apples. Somehow things had to get better in 1985.

DESPERATION DROVE ME DOWNTOWN THE first week of January. The house was empty, everyone back in college. My friend called to tell me MCI, the long-distance company she worked for that broke up AT&T, was hiring new salespeople every week. On Monday morning, I showed up at MCI's front door. And again, on Tuesday, Wednesday, and Thursday. What did I have to lose? When I went back again on Friday, they hired me. The job was to knock on doors of businesses and get them to switch from AT&T. At forty-six, I was fifteen years older than anyone else in the salesforce. The eighteen or so aggressive young men and women didn't know what to make of me. I shadowed my friend for a day or two and then struck out on my own.

"Hi, I'm Betsy Bell and I'm here to give you a long-distance option that will save your business lots of money."

In one print shop, after hearing my introduction, the owner whirled around and shouted to his staff, "You thought Ma Bell was dead? Well, she's not dead. She's here, selling MCI."

Don had no concept of sales as a career, but he was grateful for my steadily increasing commissions. Like the job or not, I had to stick with this.

March marked two years since our Tashkent trip. While Target Seattle–inspired peace groups swirled around the region, Marlow learned his medical team had no more to offer. We held a reunion in the social hall at Saint Mark's. Bloedel Hall filled with people. Marlow stood on the stage, a shadow of his former self, wearing a chemo cap where a crown of curls once haloed his face. His father supported him. The slideshow, Marlow's final creation, was the centerpiece of the evening.

In Virginia, friends and colleagues at *National Geographic* raised money to get the show televised or made into a DVD, but the technology just wasn't there to make a faithful copy. Another twenty years went by before I digitally replicated the show.

After the reunion, Marlow went home with his father. He died a month later, at age twenty-five. I felt such grief losing this beautiful young man and his extraordinary talent. His death seemed sacrificial, as though he had laid down his life for a cause. Of course, no one could know cause and effect in a cancer like his, or anyone's for that matter. It was so sad. Little did I know that Don's life would be taken by cancer in five years' time.

During his last month of life, Marlow presented the slideshow to the National Geographic Society and American University, quipping to the audience about being a guinea pig for cancer drugs. In his obituary, he was quoted as saying, "As one doctor put it, 'There are significant benefits to be gained by your participating in the study—it's just that the benefits will not necessarily accrue to you personally.' Fair enough. It beats sitting on my ass and watching the grass grow."

I took a lesson from Marlow and stayed busy at work. Before long, as I got better at selling long-distance service, my earnings topped Don's. Don was relieved, even a bit awestruck at my success, which made me happy. But the stress of competition, working for an organization I didn't believe in, and turning forty-nine and then fifty with its attendant menopause played havoc with my health.

A woman approached me at a business networking event and asked if I'd like to learn more about nutrition. I ended up changing my diet and adding her company's nutritional supplements. The changes were dramatic and nearly all the menopause symptoms disappeared. The changes in how I ate drove a wedge between Don and me.

Over the years, we had stayed connected in the kitchen, over food and drink. Early on, we'd drink sherry while I cooked. As I got busier, he played with recipes. By the time I worked for MCI, he did most of the food preparation in our house. Now I wanted a simple diet with less butter, meat, bread, and cheese. I wasn't willing to eat his rich foods anymore. Oh, how I wanted it to make no difference if I drank water while he drank wine. But I felt I was losing the essence of our relationship to gain health.

We still camped, hiked, and backpacked every chance we got. And snuggled in our sleeping bag on remote mountain meadows and beaches on Washington's coast. With summer came our Uzbek guest, the first visiting professor from Tashkent State University. We gave Goga Igoyatov Priscilla's old room while Priscilla stayed in Olympia to work. Ruth, Eleanor, and another college student lived on the third floor, working summer jobs. Grace lived with a boyfriend.

I'd been eager to host an Uzbek to bring the friendship experience home. The history professor was a slight, olive-skinned man in his mid-forties with slick, black hair and skittery black eyes. If he spoke English, I wasn't aware.

I said to Don, "He reads the *New York Times* from cover to cover. But won't speak to me."

Don accepted that this was a cultural thing. Every day, professor Igoyatov came home in the early afternoon and sat reading at the round kitchen table in the little breakfast room, glancing at the front door. When I tried to engage him, he shrugged his shoulders, turned away, and said, "I wait for Professor Bell."

I'd come in from the challenges of getting a few new MCI customers to prepare fresh vegetables, salads, and summer fruits. Our guest hardly touched them, eating only meat and bread and drinking volumes of black tea loaded with sugar. The entire month he lived with us, he never gave me any of his clothes to launder. His body odor assailed me when I came near him. I secretly wished the month would end.

Finally, I remembered that on our trip in 1983 some of us had had dinner in the home of a Tashkent State professor. The only women in the living room that night were Americans. At one point, I stuck my head into the kitchen where our host's wife and a couple of her friends prepared our meal. These women were all professional and at least one was a college teacher herself. Uzbek women did not mingle socially with their men. Our Uzbek guest was doing his best in Seattle. Four short weeks were not enough time to bridge that cultural gap. Fifteen years earlier, I would have naturally kept my wifely place. Now, I wanted this man from Uzbekistan to experience an independent woman as an equal. I was unable or unwilling to accept the differences and felt like a failure in my effort to welcome the stranger into our home.

In the spring of 1986, Eleanor graduated from Bryn Mawr and then Grace graduated from Evergreen. Eleanor was home briefly in the summer before heading to Berkeley for graduate school. Grace lived with her boyfriend in Seattle, Priscilla stayed in Olympia, and Ruth came home for another summer of working, hiking with friends, occasionally participating with Target Seattle spin-off groups, and helping us entertain visiting Soviets.

One early fall day, I opened the front door to over fifty schoolteachers from Russia. I had completely forgotten I'd offered our house as Plan B in case of a rained-out picnic in the arboretum just down the street from us. The Seattle host volunteers rushed to set up a feast of fried chicken and coleslaw and potato salad while I scrambled to set up extra chairs and fill water pitchers. Our large living room overflowed with smiling educators. My smile was tentative. I was so grateful Ruth was there to help mediate the confusion I felt. How could I resent these visitors and a chance to show them hospitality? Didn't I want these peace actions? What had changed?

I wasn't happy with my attitude toward Don either. The more he busied himself with the various committees' activities, the more I sniped at him for not pushing for full professor. It wasn't his ambition. He didn't value academic research and thought most history journals were full of esoteric material fit only for other academics. He never had been interested in publishing solely for the sake of advancement. Why did I expect him to be now? He taught because he loved his students and imparting knowledge. That made me fall in love with him so many years earlier. He made the historic past an adventure. Excellence in teaching was his aspiration, not dry analysis.

His best teaching was an off-campus study group in the classics with a handpicked group of undergraduates—a kind of great books seminar of ideas. I was jealous of their discussions of Plato and Aristotle and torn between my push for independence and wanting to belong to his inner circle. I was once the center of Don's circle. Then, I made the choice to leave. A new circle called me, one that didn't and couldn't include Don—women who followed a Wiccan path to celebrate the Solstices, Equinox, and lesser Sabbats, the cycle of life and death.

Our drift apart bothered me so much, I sought a counselor to help me stay connected in my marriage while becoming independent. Our physical bond was intense and satisfying. Divorce was not an option.

While Don continued to balance teaching with Russian peace partnership activities—becoming chair of the Seattle-Tashkent Sister City Committee, speaking on behalf of the Peace Park being built in Tashkent—I buried myself in work to try to find my own balance. I'd decided to become an independent distributor of the supplements I found so helpful in addition to my MCI work. The MCI sales experience made it easy for me to make appointments with potential vitamin customers. Don recognized my happiness at finding something that resonated so deeply with my core values—taking responsibility for one's own health and an opportunity for women to have an independent income while staying home to care for their families. He was grateful for the changes that had come over me, but didn't want my income to drop. Maybe we'd found a way for our circles to overlap, not eclipse each other. I no longer swung like a pendulum between hot and cold, energetic and falling asleep, no longer sniped at him for nothing.

The fall of 1987, we spent a few days in Chaco Canyon on the way home from our annual trip to the Texas panhandle to visit Don's mother. We loved the southwest and traveled back year after year. Our tent at the base of the western rock outcropping faced the monument in the center of the powerful lay lines extending across the valley. A full moon set off the coyotes, whose yips and howls kept us awake, listening to the night. The next day we hiked to the outer edges of the ancient track, climbing a mesa to an Anasazi outstation. Returning to the campsite through the thick dew of a damp draw at the base of the mesa, Don parted tall reeds and grasses so we could follow the darkening path. Insects swarmed around us. One bit Don on his ankle. The bite smarted and the area swelled immediately. In the light of my headlamp, the bite was deep and long. In the morning, his ankles, knees, and hips were swollen and sore. He could barely crawl out of the tent.

Nevertheless, he was determined to visit Hovenweep monument, a few miles away. The air was like a blast furnace. We left our car and got as far as a cottonwood before he collapsed. I rushed back for a camp chair and then to the ranger station. The ranger helped me get Don to the cool of the visitor center, took one look at the bite and pulled out his walkie-talkie. He radioed the hospital in Cortez and told them we were coming. My heart pounded the entire hour drive back. Don underwent five hours of tests while I wandered the town thinking about all the insect bites he'd gotten over the thirty years I had known him, including stings on the jugular when trying to move a bee hive in extreme Kansas heat—our doctor showed up minutes after I called then and administered the epinephrine that probably saved his life.

This time, the specialists discharged Don from the hospital, and he said little about the conversation with the doctors. The test results would be sent to University Family Medicine, available when we got home. We decided to cut our trip short. I drove to Canyonlands National Park for one more night in a campground, fixed dinner by lantern light, and helped him into bed. His every joint hurt. In the morning, I went on a short hike. The large white boulders glowed in the dawn as I scrambled up the worn groove made by hundreds of feet before me. I couldn't bear that Don wouldn't share this with me. Back at camp, I begged him to make the effort. He did, stifling groans and catching his breath from the pain of climbing up that mountainous rock.

The vacation was over. The medication administered at the hospital hadn't made a dent in the swelling of his joints. I packed us up and drove north, stopping once at a motel during the twenty-hour trip. We filled the silence with cassette tapes of Mozart, Bach, Vivaldi, Brahms, Sibelius, and Beethoven. Selfish thoughts of losing our last shared pleasure filled me with dread. I couldn't imagine how he suffered, sitting with every joint swollen.

At home, the doctor at Family Medicine looked at the lab test results, but we didn't talk about them. The swelling went down, but Don stopped jogging, and our walks in the arboretum were slower and less frequent. I worked my two sales jobs, comparing the cultures of the two companies. I was getting close to leaving MCI. It was another year before I earned a car and a big enough income in direct selling to quit the phone company completely.

Meanwhile, Gorbachev came to power in the USSR. His policy of glasnost opened the floodgates to more and more travel and exchanges. He pardoned a Russian nuclear physicist, Andrei Sakharov, who had been put under house arrest by Andropov. Sakharov influenced the new Soviet leader's position on the Strategic Arms Reduction Treaty. The US-proposed arms limitations were accepted by the Russian negotiating team. I liked to think Uncle Tom knew this fellow nuclear scientist and his work on human rights, but we never discussed it.

Don stayed closely connected to each and every one of the peace projects going to the USSR. His off-campus seminars continued often in our dining room. I disappeared into my sales office and made phone calls. The counselor I was seeing helped me accept our different paths. I didn't need to host his seminars or prepare tea and cookies for his students. I didn't need to feel guilty about doing my own thing in a different part of the house. We could learn to share our days and appreciate each other's lives between the sheets, after the lights were out. It was easier said than done. It was uncomfortable to drop the role I had accepted with the marriage vows at age nineteen, thirty-one years earlier. More than uncomfortable. I felt tortured, split down the middle.

In the spring, Ruth graduated from college. Her internship moved right into full-time work in recycling, Seattle's experimental approach to reducing waste. Priscilla graduated. She had developed a business as a group exercise trainer with a big following in Olympia. Both girls had serious boyfriends and no longer came home to live. Grace was engaged to be married and worked for a businessman. Eleanor was well into her PhD program in Sociology at UC Berkeley.

In March of 1989, I left MCI, confident that I could earn what we needed now that the girls were out of college. One of the first results of perestroika was a visit to Seattle by the diocesan archbishop of the Russian Orthodox church, Metropolitan Alexy. Don threw himself into planning and preparation, pressing all my dutiful wife trigger points. It wasn't pretty.

Metropolitan Alexy came to Seattle as part of the second delegation of the Leningrad-Seattle Sister Churches Program. Don volunteered to prepare a lavish Russian meal for the reception, held in one of Seattle's local churches. Single-handedly, he worked in our small kitchen fixing food for about one hundred people.

"Are you doing this huge meal alone?" I challenged him. "Don't you have a committee? Helpers lined up?" He said nothing, just scrubbed potatoes and set big pots of water to boil. For years, I'd pitched in when he planned gala events, but not this time. I hadn't signed up for this. He put a hand on his lower back and leaned against the stovetop. I sighed, grabbed a dishtowel and began wiping down counters, then helped load our platters, serving spoons, and large bowls of elaborate Russian dishes into our old, two-door Datsun. The backseat was filled with cases of wine and sparkling water. Silent, we drove to the church. He unloaded the food and carried it up a long flight of stairs. I wrenched the cases of wine out of the back seat, felt a searing pain shoot down my leg, took a deep breath, and charged up those stairs. Back down for two more boxes, in terrible pain. In the social hall, several friends he'd recruited waited to help transfer the food onto platters and promised to stay to clean up after the reception. I took the bus home, lay down with ice and anti-inflammatories, and fumed my way to sleep.

Don came home hours later to a messy kitchen and slid quietly into bed. The next morning, my first steps downstairs confirmed the worst: I had possibly herniated a disc. I lay on the living room floor unable to move. Don heard my cry for help and got me to a comfortable position, called my massage therapist, and drove me to chiropractor and physical therapist appointments until I could function again. I cursed myself for lifting that box in a state of rage.

On Christmas morning, all four daughters were home. We sat in front of the living room fireplace, drinking tea and eating traditional Swedish apricot loaf.

Priscilla noticed first.

"Daddy, you're shivering."

Grace reached out her hand to touch his cheek. "You're flaming hot."

"What's happening, sweetheart?" I asked.

His teeth chattered. He tried to stand but sunk back into the couch, pulling the afghan around him. "Everything hurts."

"I'm taking you to the hospital," I said. He didn't protest. The girls helped him into the front seat. I drove a few blocks to University Hospital's emergency room. They took a blood draw and were back in what seemed like seconds. They put him in a wheelchair and took him to a room immediately. Hot blankets, warm water to drink, and the promise of an on-call family medicine doctor in half an hour.

"I'm fine. So sorry to ruin Christmas like this. Betsy, go home to the girls and tell them I'll be alright."

"You sure?"

"There's nothing more you can do here. They'll be worried sick. Go."

I was already worried sick myself, but did as he told. The girls had cleared the tea and were dressed, insisting on going to the hospital immediately. When we got to Don's room, a nurse stopped us and handed all five of us gowns and masks. I couldn't believe the notice posted on his door: Special Protective Isolation.

Don was sick with what the doctors at the University of Washington medical center thought might be the precursor to leukemia. His white blood cell count was a fraction of normal. His doctor offered no treatment other than antibiotics. A protocol existed for treating an aggressive form of leukemia, but Don's condition didn't call for chemo—yet. Our doctor drove to the hospital from his home in Kirkland, interrupting his own family Christmas, to discuss Don's weakened immune state, and discharged him into our care. "He's better off at home. Too much disease in the hospital. Wash your hands and keep any sick person from visiting."

Before he left, he looked at Don's chart and asked about the vitamins listed there. "No vitamins. Nothing but food. Come to my office next week and we'll discuss your situation further." Then he took Don's hand in his, and added in a voice heavy with emotion, "Have a Merry Christmas."

Merry Christmas, indeed. I pushed down the panic that threatened to bring up breakfast. It was time to put on armor and prepare for war. Our daughters would coddle him. I was going to study this disease and meet it head on. What could I do without the help of my trusted vitamins?

DON'S FEVER BROKE, ASSISTED BY antibiotics, lots of hot tea, broth, and rest. But his white cell count hovered around 600, well below the normal range of 4,500–10,000. I read everything I could get my hands on, and learned that the diagnosis of leukemia they anticipated from his blood work meant death in two and a half years with or without treatment. Over the next two years, I prepared macrobiotic meals at home and drove Don to every alternative medicine therapy I could find, from energy healing to chelation. He humored me by going to multiple appointments, but refused to undergo IV infusions. Since I, too, was skeptical of the chelation research methods and results, I didn't push.

Don felt well enough to teach winter quarter and miraculously did not catch a cold or the flu despite an unchanged, low white blood cell count. He began a second home seminar at the request of many friends and fellow members of the original Target Seattle steering committee. Every few weeks, attendees gathered around our dining table and listened to Don discuss the historic background of the current shifts in Russia and Eastern Europe.

The many changes that occurred that winter gave them plenty to discuss. Gorbachev's decision to loosen the Soviet yoke on the countries of Eastern Europe led to the collapse of the Berlin Wall in November 1989, just before Don's illness. The overthrow of Communist rule throughout Eastern Europe followed. We had a new president in the White House, George H. Bush. Bush let events unfold organically, careful not to do anything to worsen Gorbachev's position. The two leaders met in early December 1989 and laid the groundwork for finalizing START negotiations. Bush encouraged Gorbachev's reform efforts, hoping the Soviet leader would succeed in shifting the USSR toward a democratic system and a market-oriented economy. Everyone watched as Gorbachev jockeyed with Boris Yeltsin to lead the dissolution of the Union of Soviet Republics.

In Seattle, plans rushed forward for the 1990 Goodwill Games, organized by Bob Walsh, and sponsored for the third time by Ted Turner, founder of CNN, who believed in the power of international sporting competitions to prevent war. The games gave Soviet and American athletes a chance to meet at a time when the Kremlin and White House used athletes as pawns in the Cold-War chess game just as they used the Russian Jews.

Don offered our home to several visitors from Russia. He wasn't going to let his suppressed immune function prevent full participation in the activities surrounding the games. My anxiety over his health smoldered and boiled between care and rage. Somehow, I kept my business going in the moments between his health appointments and Russian-related events. I chauffeured six men in a rented van on a sightseeing tour, ending at Seattle's most prestigious restaurant parking lot, Canlis, where I let them all out before returning the car. During the several hours–long drive, I had been invisible, pointing out this and that, but never included in the spirited conversation. I told Ruth, not Don, of my frustration.

IN AUGUST, RUTH, ELEANOR, AND I left a house full of Russians and hiked the Wonderland Trail around Mt. Rainier. My doctors and therapist prepared me for the ninety-five-mile hike. The eight days of climbing ridges and descending glacial-fed rivers were among the most memorable of my life. We left the mountain after sixty-five miles due to a violent hailstorm. Eight years later, Ruth and I finished hiking the remaining thirty miles.

We returned in time for the opening of the Goodwill Games in Husky Stadium. Ruth, Don and I stood with several dozen delegates from the USSR as Kenny G danced his way onto the field under clear blue skies. The wailing high notes of his soprano saxophone held the overflowing stadium spellbound and sent shivers down my spine. When the flags of our two countries appeared, the audience roared with applause. It was a moment of triumph for all of us who fostered friendship between our countries. Don threw his arms around me and Ruth in a fierce hug. Every ounce of me hugged them back.

After the games, it was time for Don to fulfill our university's part in the Tashkent State-University of Washington professor exchange, which meant a one-month stay for Don in Tashkent. Checking in with his doctors, we learned that his immune function was still in the tank—his white blood cell count still hovered around 600. I begged him to reconsider making the dangerous trip, but he wouldn't hear of canceling. Ruth had just left her two-year recycling job and was headed to India for several months. She was enthusiastic about returning to Tashkent and wanted to accompany her father. I was so relieved. I didn't want Don to go alone for fear he would get severely ill over there, but I didn't want to go with him to be his caretaker. I was tied in knots with anxiety about his health and furious about his insistence on going. Ruth was calm, present with no judgment, and happy to be on a trip with her dad.

Ruth confessed later she was bored much of that month in Tashkent. The social fuss the people made over us in 1983 didn't happen this time. No parties. No gaiety of shared experience with the other high-schoolers. The lectures were three hours long with pauses for translation. She absorbed Don's teaching and asked him many questions about the topic each afternoon.

A picture from the trip showed Don drinking vodka with a couple of men hunched over fishing poles on the shore of a lake, mountains reaching for the sky along the far shore. Afghanistan lay on the other side of those peaks.

When the month of teaching ended, Don and Ruth returned to London and parted ways, she to Mumbai, he to Seattle.

Upon his return, a bacterium had overwhelmed his diminished immune system. Gaunt and weakened, he still walked to the university to teach his fall classes. His stomach troubles resulted in a fistula in his colon. Without a mass of white cells, the doctors had nothing to excise. Don was miserable. He carried a doughnut-shaped pillow and lectured sitting down.

Grace and Tom Killorin married in our living room in November of 1990. Ruth came back from India early for the celebration. She and her sisters and a small group of friends witnessed their happy exchange of vows. Don's joints hurt and he could stand only long enough to present his eldest daughter to her husband before he lay down again on the couch. That morning, I'd prepared the menu he designed. Unfamiliar with the recipes, I zipped back and forth between the kitchen and the couch for instructions. In some ways, Don's illness meant I'd returned to his circle. No point in being upset about the situation. I was just getting things done.

ONCE DON'S SYSTEM CREATED A sufficient mass of infection-fighting cells, the doctors operated. Getting the infection out of his body increased his energy. More antibiotics kept him on his feet. He finished fall and winter quarters.

"Looks like leukemia, but we can't call it that until irregular stem cells are at 65 percent," the doctors said. I kept the macrobiotic foods and nasty tasting herbal teas coming.

Don barely finished reading exams for winter quarter when he took a turn for the worse. This time, his blood test revealed the dreaded diagnosis of aggressive leukemia. His doctors' enthusiasm for beginning the recommended chemotherapy was a sharp contrast to my devastation. Their strategy for combat was about to take over mine. I'd managed to push back the inevitable for two-plus years. Don was hospitalized for the treatment, out of my circle of care.

The brutal dosage of chemicals with little or no side-effect-controlling medicine dripped into his port day after day and left him sicker than before. Ruth and Grace were often at his bedside. Priscilla and her fiancé, Kevin Dahlstrom, had moved to the upstairs apartment in our house to be near. Eleanor came briefly then left to finish her required coursework for the doctorate. Don needed constant attention as his body rebelled against the cell-killing drugs. I was grateful for all the help.

It was impossible for me to sit in the hospital room and watch this man, whose dignity had defined him since the day he walked into my high school classroom, disintegrate into a mass of uncontrollable body functions. Somehow, his daughters could help him to the bathroom and clean up the inevitable messes. I showed up early during hospital rounds to hear his team discuss his case. Contradictory recommendations depending on the medical specialty drove me to demand that our general practitioner coordinate his care. I turned up again around nine thirty at night and slipped into bed beside him. Sometimes, if his suffering was too great, he didn't want to be touched.

Eleanor visited during spring break, but had to return for her final quarter. Don's treatment was over mid-May. We all waited for Don's bone marrow to produce new mother cells and a protective immune system. He couldn't leave the hospital until then. Don wanted to be at Eleanor's graduation to celebrate her academic achievement, but the doctors said "no." The rest of us left him in the hospital and drove nonstop, taking turns sleeping, to Berkeley in time to celebrate. We called him from ZaZZ, a pizza place in Oakland we'd visited every time we went to the Bay Area to see Eleanor. Don was so far away, it was heartbreaking.

Before Don left the hospital, the chairman of the History

Department came to discuss the future. Then, he changed Don's status to professor emeritus. In my heart, I knew he would never teach again, and was grateful for that dignifying title. I took over the big-picture finances, annuitizing his thirty-one years of investments through the higher-education retirement system to provide income for us, and eventually for me, after his death.

Don taught one class summer quarter, shuffling off to the university every day, the doughnut-hole pillow under his arm.

His blood cell tests came back normal, and we spent a beautiful summer in the backyard, and took a couple of trips in the area to see friends. We even made the annual Shakespeare festival in Ashland with the Bryn Mawr Club. Don lay on a picnic table at a park in Roseburg, Oregon, halfway down I-5 so I could administer a drip of medicine into his port.

Don planned the garden for fall, pouring over the Territorial Seeds catalog and ordering 1000 bulbs. He outlined a new course for fall quarter on the history of Christianity, a topic he'd lectured on casually for many years, usually as adult education offerings in church.

Eleanor left Seattle for Cornell University in upstate New York to begin her teaching career in September. A kind of euphoria wrapped everyone in the family and all who loved Don when they spent time with him that summer. He was so enthusiastic about the future. Some others may have watched and waited each day for the cancer to come back. I certainly could not relax into the healthy present, but persisted in making marketing appointments and increasing my sales volume, hedging against a solitary future. We didn't talk about cancer.

Don abandoned all attempts at a healing diet, instead cooking rich pastas with every sauce imaginable—clam, smoked salmon, three-cheese, and the one I loved, primavera. He poured neat, single-malt scotch, or a gin and tonic to begin our evening meal preparations. He and one or the other of his daughters went out to eat at favorite restaurants several times a week.

His history seminars continued. Friends and Target Seattle companions discussed the further unraveling of the Soviet Union. In a piece published in the Seattle-Tashkent News, Don wrote about how difficult it was to keep "in touch with our Tashkent friends despite all the governmental hostility and confusing rhetoric by both US and Soviet authorities. I have a hunch that citizen-to-citizen contacts may be more important now than during the Cold War, but we are currently more confused by speeding developments and the blizzard of questions." He was afraid the internal Uzbekistan turmoil might turn bloody. Unrest and even civil war erupted in several of the fifteen states that had made up the USSR. Don conducted the evening seminars with a big classroom map and extensive background histories of each state.

Eleanor wanted Don to visit her in Ithaca before her classes started. Before buying a ticket, he went for a check-up. The cancer was back, full-blown and aggressive. His medical team advised a more forceful treatment. He and I talked about the possibility of waiting to begin until after he visited Eleanor. Reason took over. What if he became seriously ill and couldn't return. She had to be ready for her classes. The risk of nontreatment was too great.

The medicine was harder on his body this time than the previous round. He lay depleted from the killing drugs as we crowded his hospital room to watch the election returns. A fellow Rhodes scholar, Bill Clinton, won. Don was too far away in his own cancer-fighting world to cheer with the rest of us. A few days later, his medical team confessed that there was nothing left to do for him. Don asked to be unplugged from all their machines and taken home.

Word spread fast that Don had come home to die. Eleanor returned from New York. Good friends came over and called everyone on our personal and my business rolodexes. The house filled with well-wishers. The girls and I stayed upstairs in the master bedroom, talking, telling stories, comforting Don. He'd come home with twenty morphine tablets, refusing to take any so he could be present as, one by one, students, colleagues, fellow citizen activists, and church members entered the room, sat by his bed and thanked him for his particular gifts to them—encouragement, leadership, inspiration, knowledge.

I had a difficult task and let this wake roll on without my supervision. I'd promised Don to help him take his own life. He didn't want the same excruciating suffering he'd witnessed with his father. He talked to each daughter explaining his decision. He would wait until Monday morning, after Eleanor's birthday.

Checking in with friends in the gay community and the Hemlock Society, I had what I needed to prepare a lethal cocktail. Don toasted us all with Laphroaig single-malt scotch and morphine, then died painlessly several hours later. It was November 16, 1992. Our family doctor came over to personally sign the death certificate so there would be no autopsy. Everyone left me in a now empty house before I called the funeral home. When the two men came, I watched them zip his body into their bag. The wall kept me on my feet. They disappeared down the stairs with him and out to the waiting hearse. I felt defeated and alone.

I HAD NO TIME TO grieve. Don's funeral was a standing-room-only celebration of all the important areas of his very public life. Nothing was said of his family life.

A month after Don died, Priscilla and Kevin married at Lakeside Academy chapel. One of Don's best friends, close to our family in Kansas and Washington, walked Priscilla down the aisle.

I was alone now in a six-thousand-square-foot Victorian/Tudor brick mansion, mortgaged to the hilt to send our daughters to college and fund our peace efforts. Who was I after thirty-five years of marriage? Promoting Marlow's Target Seattle slideshow had been my project. Then, needing to generate a substantial income, I'd created a career in sales, something I could do while remaining a supportive wife, and that sustained me socially as well as financially. I was grateful for my business.

Dissolving the structure of a thirty-five-year marriage took a lot of effort and kept me from the work of grieving. Then, one day, I came home from a walk and found one of our kitties dead on the sidewalk. I picked up her stiff body and carried her home, then set her on the step while I got a shovel from the garage. As I dug a hole in the yard to bury her, I started wailing and couldn't stop, keening like a woman who'd lost her whole village. The little black adventuress Princess was dead. The university, the center of our lives for twenty-three years, was anathema to me. Don had given his life to make the institution more relevant to civil society. Leadership in Target Seattle expressed this conviction. It had not served him well. I wanted nothing to do with any of it. I'd rejected Saint Mark's and did not look there for comfort. Only Wildman, a sweet tabby, was left to wander the many-roomed house with me.

Before January was over, I found students to rent the empty bedrooms, then converted the dining room to a retail store that carried all the items that brought others and me well-being. One day the following winter, I sat at my desk and looked into the garden, shaking my head at the foolish blossoms of the *Autumnalis*. For twenty-five years I had growled at this overarching tree which seemed to mock winter's death, blooming in December. This time, the frothy white petals made me smile. They promised renewal.

I NEVER FOUND OUT IF the refusenik families received our letters. I'll never know how much influence Target Seattle had in ending the threat of nuclear war or in breaking down borders between people of different cultures, but the act of taking the People to People slide show around the country broke down my own insecurities. I was sad, but not overcome by grief. It didn't happen overnight. It took four years for me to dispose of Don's library and all his effects and sell the house. Even as I started life anew, I had the sense that if Don had lived, somehow overcoming cancer, he and I would have spent the rest of our married life as a team comprised of two equal people, each contributing our ideas, our values, our dreams with mutual respect. The physical tenderness that undergirded our marriage would have continued to grow and nourish us. I would be as independent and self-assured in our marriage as I felt as a new widow. With him or without him, I stood strong.

Four Essays

I have included four essays. Each is a personal account that further illustrates the intention and impact of our citizen initiative. While I chose these four essays to illustrate the reach of Target Seattle, many other essays have been written by various participants. Collecting them in their own volume would constitute a history of a time when ordinary citizens were transformed into agents of peace.

Dr. Roscius N. Doan is a retired physician who learned Russian and lived and worked in Tashkent as part of the early exchange programs. Written in 1987, Doan reflects on the unlikely pairing of two very different cities under the auspices of Sister Cities International, created at President Eisenhower's 1956 White House conference on citizen diplomacy. Eisenhower envisioned an organization that could be the hub of peace and prosperity by creating bonds between people from different cities around the world. By forming these relationships, President Eisenhower reasoned that people of different cultures could celebrate and appreciate their differences and build partnerships that would lessen the chance of new conflicts. Nearly twenty years later, Seattle's pairing with Tashkent was the first and most successful US/USSR sister city relationship.

The Seattle-Tashkent Connection: An Account of a Successful Sister-City Pairing

By Dr. Roscius N. Doan

Some may ask, whatever do Seattle and Tashkent have in common? What does a 135-year-old city share with a city that has 2,003 years of recorded history? What is the link between a green, wet north Pacific seaport and an arid, landlocked central Asian metropolis on ancient caravan routes? How is a Western city of the American superpower related to an Eastern city of the Soviet superpower? The answer is we are sister cities.

How did this unlikely pairing take place? In August 1971, the mayors of Tashkent, Irkutsk, and Sochi visited Seattle as part of a promotional tour by Alaska Airlines. It seems that the Tashkenters and the Seattleites hit it off. A Seattle-Tashkent Sister City Committee was formed. The result was that in 1972, the mayors exchanged letters of invitation to establish the first Soviet-American sister-city affiliation. On January 22, 1973, the Seattle City Council passed Resolution 23992, adopting Tashkent as a sister city of Seattle. Within the year, official delegations had been exchanged. In 1974, in honor of the visit of the Tashkent mayor and his delegation, Seattle inaugurated Tashkent Park, a half-acre on Boylston Street East, between East Republican and East Mercer Avenues. Since that time, numerous official and semiofficial groups have been enthusiastically received by the mayors' offices in both Seattle and Tashkent.

The early years of the relationship were spent visiting each other, getting acquainted. We Americans, at least, started from a fairly low baseline of knowledge. We Seattleites at first thought we had a Russian sister city. Our first learning was that Tashkent is in fact an Uzbek city. "Uzbek?" we asked. "What's that?" The Uzbeks are the third-largest ethnic group in the Soviet Union, trailing only the Russians and Ukrainians. They are a Muslim people who speak a Turkic language, Uzbek. Tashkent is the capital of the Uzbek Soviet Socialist Republic, which borders Afghanistan in Soviet Central Asia. It is a rapidly growing city of over two million, the Soviet Union's fourth-largest city. It may reach four million by the year 2000. "Wow! Uzbek and Muslim. In Communist Russia, you say?" "No, in the Union of Soviet Socialist Republics." "Oh . . . " And so it went.

Slowly, Seattleites began to appreciate the richness of Uzbek culture. We gained some insight into the complexities of contemporary Soviet life within which that culture is expressed. Early, we were delighted by Uzbek national dancing. In 1980, the famous Bakhor Dance Ensemble visited Seattle and performed. Seattle's own Tanavar Dance Ensemble, which presents dances of Uzbekistan, has benefited from the tutelage of Uzbek national artists. In 1985, the director of Tanavar, Laurel Gray, traveled to Tashkent, where she received further instruction.

By the early 1980s, the Seattle-Tashkent Sister City Committee held festivals honoring official visitors from Tashkent. On February 4, 1982, Mayor Royer proclaimed Tashkent Day to celebrate our sister-city relationship. That relationship seemed ready for more. How did the sister cities fit into the larger context of contention between the superpowers?

We began to share common problems. In the fall of 1982, a consortium of community peace groups presented a nine-day citywide educational event, called Target Seattle, on the prevention of nuclear war. One activity of that event was the drafting of a letter to the people of Tashkent. The letter was an expression of concern about nuclear war and a call for our nations to work together to prevent it. This bilingual Russian-English letter was published in petition form and made available for signing at all Target Seattle events. Community groups and churches also canvassed neighborhoods for signatures. Forty-two thousand signatures were collected on two thousand copies of the letter. The mayor of Seattle and the city council signed the first copy, which was sent to the mayor of Tashkent. We informed the official Soviet Peace Committee of the letter. Following Target Seattle, we expressed our desire to the Tashkent mayor to send a delegation to our sister city to deliver the letters in person. The Soviet response was overwhelmingly favorable. A delegation of thirty-two of us paid our own way to the Soviet Union in March of 1983. We were warmly received in Moscow, Samarkand, Tashkent, and Leningrad. In Tashkent, the mayor extended the very best of Soviet Uzbek hospitality to our group. We came with a simple message of peace, and they responded with great cordiality.

The Tashkent response was immediate. Within a month of our group's return to Seattle, nearly 120,000 Tashkenters had signed a letter of peace to the people of Seattle. The letter concluded, "While admitting that we do have differences, we nevertheless think we are united in pursuing the great cause: the lofty goal of mankind's salvation." The superpower signature race was accelerating.

The educational impact on Seattle in the aftermath of that trip was significant, as we returned to report back to our own constituencies and accepted invitations to share our experiences. A moving slide presentation of that trip, prepared by the late Marlow Boyer of our delegation, was shown to thousands in the Seattle area. Marlow edited an expanded portrait of Seattle and Tashkent, *City to City*, before his untimely death. That production is cherished in the two cities. It was reformatted in 16 mm sound film and has been distributed internationally.

The cadence of Seattle-Tashkent relations was temporarily set back later that year when a Korean Air Lines flight was tragically shot down [by Soviet jet fighters]. The scheduled visit of the Seattle mayor to Tashkent that month to celebrate Tashkent's two thousandth anniversary was canceled.

In retrospect, 1983 seems like a turning point in local Soviet-American activities. That fall, Target Seattle continued with the theme "Soviet Realities." For nine days, all aspects of Soviet life and its relationship to us were discussed. The sister-city relationship was both a stimulus for, and the recipient of, energies from Target Seattle. Within the next couple of years, a number of new organizations appeared in the Seattle area with a focus on Soviet-American relations. A network of synergetic efforts enriched all our projects. As groups would go to Tashkent from Seattle, we would carry each other's messages.

The exchange of official delegations continued apace. In September 1984, Mayor Royer led a delegation to Tashkent. An accompanying TV crew from station KOMO produced a documentary of the sister-city relationship entitled *Cold War, Warm Hearts*. The two cities were evolving a model of Soviet-American interaction.

Tashkent Mayor Shukurulla Mirsayidov brought a delegation to Seattle in September 1985. The mayors talked of citizen exchanges. Mirsayidov left an exhibit of Soviet school books, uniforms, and school satchels for the little school house at the Seattle Children's Museum in Seattle Center. The Tashkent delegates got to know their Seattle professional counterparts in informal gatherings. Together, we explored the possibilities for new projects. A high point was a concert in the Fifth Avenue Theater attended by three thousand, featuring noted Uzbek musicians and dancers and the Seattle Peace Chorus.

In January 1986, Ploughshares, an organization of former Peace Corps volunteers working for peace, took a delegation to the Soviet Union. We had eight school-age delegates with us. In Tashkent, sister-school relationships were established with four Tashkent schools. There in the schools, Seattle and Tashkent children folded paper cranes together as part of Ploughshares' Million Cranes Project. A slow-scan TV demonstration was pioneered there, linking Mayor Royer at the Seattle Children's Museum with Mayor Mirsayidov. Dr. Rizaev of Tashkent Hospital No. 1, who had visited Seattle the previous fall, proposed a physician exchange with Seattle. David Fenner of the University of Washington explored a student exchange with the dean of Tashkent State University.

Soviet sculptor Jakov Shapiro graciously received us at his studio for lunch. There our host emotionally informed us for the first time of the space shuttle *Challenger* disaster. The poignancy of his condolences touched us deeply. "We Soviets understand the depths of your grief, because we also have suffered our space program tragedies." Teacher Jay Sasnett of Seattle's Washington Middle School was especially moved, as he had been a state finalist in the teacher-astronaut program. Another in our delegation from the East Coast had known the teacher-astronaut Christa McAuliffe personally. The tragedy brought us together at a deeper level than we might otherwise have experienced. Shapiro then unveiled a model of a statue he proposed to donate to Seattle for Tashkent Park.

In recent months, the interaction has been quickening. A variety of joint projects appear about to unfold. These have been facilitated by a return visit to Seattle of Mirsayidov in July and trips to Tashkent in the fall by members of the Sister City Committee and Ploughshares. A new proposal has been made for the development of a Seattle gift to a park in Tashkent. Initially conceived as a tiled *Peace Path* through a park, the concept will be refined in further discussions. Fred Noland and Bob Alsdorf of Ploughshares report that Tashkent officials proposed that a Seattle cafe be opened in the park they were shown. The idea is an exciting prospect for development. A physician exchange appears likely at this writing. An art exchange is in the early stages of discussion.

One of the most exciting new directions is the sister-school activity spearheaded by Jay Sasnett. So far, six Seattle schools have been paired with four Tashkent schools. Coupling an American elementary or middle school and high school with a Soviet school seems to be an appropriate formula, as Soviet schools usually include grades one through ten. The Tashkent mayor is enthusiastic about this project. He suggested that Tashkent has "three hundred schools to go" for such an effort. In March 1987, thirty-two students from five Seattle sister schools, accompanied by ten teachers, will spend a week in Tashkent visiting their sister-school counterparts. Interest among Seattle children is keen. One hundred fifty children applied for the thirty-two slots. The student representatives will receive fifty hours of Russian and Uzbek language instruction. The potential for more and better student exchange activity seems great. The USSR has proposed a high school exchange of three hundred students, to be run by Sister Cities International. The Seattle-Tashkent Sister City Association has applied and would appear to have a head start.

What has made the Seattle-Tashkent connection a success? There are many reasons. Serendipity. Seattle had the first American sister-city relationship with the Soviet Union, and hence it is the most mature. The mayors in the two cities have been consistently supportive. In Seattle, the Sister City Committee has benefited from vigorous leadership in co-chairs Rosanne Royer and Virginia Westberg. The

Seattle community at large has fostered this activity. Organizations and individuals have been supportive.

Seattle has also benefited from Soviet Uzbek pride and initiative. In an attitude of mutual respect, both cities acknowledge their differences. Seattle honors the diversity Tashkent represents in Soviet culture, and Tashkent responds. We are both the richer for the experience.

Soviets as a whole value this relationship. It is their strongest American sister-city connection. Currently, there are six Soviet-American sister-city pairings, with ten more soon to be established. Seattle will be the site of a Soviet-American Sister City Conference in May 1987. It is hoped that the mayors of the paired cities will attend.

The Seattle-Tashkent sister-city relationship is one approach to long-term education and citizen diplomacy. A constituency of caring, informed citizens with multidimensional experiences of the Soviet Union can be built from this and similar American-Soviet activities. Out of this constituency may come more creative ideas and fresh initiatives that will ultimately lead to change in the macropolitics of the superpower confrontation. Seen in this way, the Seattle-Tashkent connection is getting down to the business of being human beings.

"Target Seattle" Revisited: 25th Anniversary of Seattle Petitioning Sister City Tashkent in the USSR for Peace, was first published by Craig Justice as a blog post. Justice was a young journalist when he traveled with the Target Seattle peace letter-carrying group in the spring of 1983. His twenty-five-year retrospective asks a question of all of us who participated in the citizen diplomacy of the eighties: Where are we now? How have our lives been shaped by that small group effort, an effort Margaret Meade named as the only thing that would ever change the world?

"Target Seattle" Revisited: 25th Anniversary of Seattle Petitioning Sister City Tashkent in the USSR for Peace

By Craig Justice

In March 1983, a group from Seattle traveled to the Soviet Union carrying five thousand petitions with over forty-two thousand signatures calling for residents of Seattle and its sister city Tashkent to work together to prevent nuclear war. The petition and the trip were offspring of a citywide teach-in called Target Seattle the year before, which brought together US government officials, scholars, experts, clergy, and citizens for a weeklong series of seminars on US-Soviet relations. Although critics complained speakers represented the liberal left, I remember attending sessions that included strong conservative speakers, such as the leading negotiator for the strategic arms limitation agreements, Undersecretary of State Richard Burt, Jeanne Kilpatrick (UN representative of the Reagan administration), balanced by those who represented the views of the peace movement. Moreover, one gentleman spoke about the benefits of a space-based missile defense system, which President Reagan announced in detail to the general public while the Seattle group was in the USSR (much to the surprise of the group as their Soviet guests asked them to comment on the subject!).

A twenty-fifth anniversary gives an excuse to pause and reflect on the trip. Was it naïve? What good, if any, came out of it? And most importantly, what has become of the participants? It's also an excuse to search through the garage and dust off the slides taken by Marlow

Boyer, son of a *National Geographic* photographer, who learned the art of photography from his father and documented the trip with outstanding photographs. Let's first revisit those times, starting in 1980. Jimmy Carter is President. The era is referred to as *détente* as the US and USSR hold discussions on limiting nuclear arms production through the SALT (strategic arms limitation treaty) process and cooperation in other fields through CSCE (Committee on Security and Cooperation in Europe). On the other hand, the Soviet Union has recently invaded Afghanistan; moreover, as a provocation to NATO (which at this time is just fifteen nations), the USSR has modernized its midrange nuclear missiles in Europe with SS-20 rockets, which are capable of reaching any European capital. As a response to the Soviet threat, NATO makes the decision to upgrade its medium-range missiles as a deterrent to the Soviet threat. The Atlantic Alliance takes a strong, unified position and will not be divided. Some of the citizenry within NATO's membership, however, have different ideas. In the summer of 1980 in Copenhagen, students—numbering in the thousands, but not a multitude—gather to begin a peaceful protest march to Paris against the missile modernization. (Of course, there are no demonstrations inside the Iron Curtain.) The Green Party—supporting environmental issues and peace through nonviolent civil disobedience—is on the rise in Germany and will soon clear a 5 percent hurdle in the polls to gain recognition in parliament as an official political party. Ronald Reagan is elected president, dousing fuel on the fires being stirred by the European Left. His words against the "Evil Empire" raise concerns among Europeans who fear becoming a battlefield in a so-called limited nuclear war between the US and the Soviet Union. On October 10, 1981, a coalition of over three hundred thousand students, trade unionists, Greens, pacifists, and concerned citizens take to the streets in Bonn (the West German capital) in peaceful protest. The silent majority in Europe does what it does best—remains silent—as the activists gain attention and make waves. There are stirrings of a similar nature in the US: the old anti–Vietnam War protesters and coalitions awaken as Reagan's rhetoric generates concerns about a nuclear holocaust. Even Petra Kelly—one of the spokespeople for the German Green Party (whose father was an American soldier) —travels to Los Angeles to address a rock concert for "peace" held at the Rose

Bowl. (From my observation, the main draw to that event was seeing the likes of Stevie Wonder, Bob Dylan, and other stars appear on stage in the spring sunshine of 1982).

In August 1982, the USS *Ohio*—the first Trident class submarine—makes its maiden home port call to Bremerton, Washington—across Puget Sound from Seattle—with enough firepower, it is claimed, to destroy the world. It is another lightning rod in the debate on how best to keep the peace (through how much strength?), and becomes a focal point for the Seattle peace movement. In Seattle, a group of citizens from over sixty organizations including church activists, the media, civic groups, nongovernmental organizations, and academia decides to put on a community symposium—coordinated by the Metropolitan YMCA in September through October, called Target Seattle—to better inform the public about US-Soviet history, foreign relations, and Russian culture and to study the consequences of nuclear war. Seattle has sister-city ties with Tashkent, the capital of Uzbekistan, located in central Asia (which is now in the news as one of the fronts against the war on terror and dealing with Afghan drug lords). One of the topics addressed by Target Seattle is "what can you as a citizen do?" One group comes up with the idea of the petition. Over thirty thousand signatures are collected. Permission is given to bring the petitions to Tashkent, with stops in Moscow and Samarkand on the way and a final stop in Leningrad before leaving.

One's opinion of the trip to the USSR at that time depended largely on one's ideological frame of reference. For those with a hardline view, the trip was seen as no good and could only serve Soviet propaganda efforts. The Seattle FBI certainly took interest in it. For those going—no one was naïve or expected political breakthroughs—it was an opportunity to further educate themselves and to try and foster more dialog between people. This delegation included the good earth of Seattle citizenry. It was not a political delegation headed by the mayor and full of politicians on a political junket, although the delegation included the wife of a future congressman (Virginia McDermott). It represented an eclectic mix of Seattle citizenry, including the director of the municipal league (Kay Bullitt), a school teacher (Linda Straley), a cancer doctor (Hugh Straley), a travel agent, a university professor and Rhodes Scholar and his family (Aldon, Elisabeth, and Ruth

Bell), a graduate college student (Mary Reichert, who had majored in Russian and was the group's unofficial interpreter and secret weapon— who could sing folk songs in Russian and recite verses from Pushkin and disarm any Soviet official with her charm), a pediatrician (Rosh Doan), an agronomist (Roy Wiebe), a photographer (Marlow Boyer), a minister who served as Pacific Northwest regional director of the Congregational church and his son (James and Jon Halfaker), an engineer (Paul Cooke), an insurance salesman (Nick Licata), and others, including a journalist (Craig Justice).

My career would take me away from Seattle to Japan and working with Asia Pacific countries before settling, of all places, in California (a land loathed by Seattleites at the time). One regret in my life is losing touch with this group. With the power of e-mail and blogs, let's see if this post will flush out and bring back others who were on this trip, so that memories and lessons learned may be shared.

Since the breakup of the Soviet Empire, the corruption of Uzbekistan's rulers has come to light.   One wonders what the hell was really going on in that country when we visited twenty-five years ago and ate caviar, downed vodka toasts, and dined on lamb pilaf with our hosts. How about the religious leader, the *grand mufti* Amim Hatib, whom we met outside of Samarkand? I remember him speaking about the importance of peace to his faith—what has happened to him and his madrassa since the fall of communism and the right to practice Islam openly?

How about the In-Tourist guide Vladimir who accompanied us? What became of him?

When the butterfly flaps its wings in Seattle, the wind stirs in Beijing. Did this peace voyage prevent a nuclear war? Of course not. Did a group of citizens better educate themselves? Absolutely! Did they become better citizens of the world for it? Let's find out.

In November after the trip, many in the group helped organize a nine-day series of lectures, workshops, and drama called "Target Seattle: Soviet Realities." The focus this time was on the Soviet Union, and included twenty-two well-informed speakers representing different views who debated the Soviet military threat, US policy options, and negotiating strategies while describing political, social, and economic conditions in the USSR. "We are asking a very great deal of our citizens—to confront the issues," said Don Bell, Target Seattle's chairman who had led the trip to Tashkent earlier in the year. As part of that program, on a Sunday evening, a few thousand residents gathered in more than 550 homes across the city to discuss their perceptions of the Soviet Union, and actions that they could take as individuals to reduce the threat of nuclear war. They met again one week later. According to Bell, Target Seattle inspired similar, though smaller, events in a dozen other communities including Vancouver, Canada; Birmingham, Alabama; and Hartford, Connecticut.

In the years that followed, Seattle and Tashkent exchanged several delegations at the mayoral level and the people-to-people level, which are described by delegation member Dr. Rosh Doan.

Now let us praise famous men and women, the ordinary people of that delegation who lived their lives and accomplished magnificent things, who, it seems, were taken away from us before their time. First was Marlow Boyer, the photographer, who put together a multimedia slide show of the trip (this was long before Al Gore and I had invented the LCD projector which would have made the enterprise much easier). Marlow wrote in his will that when he died, he hoped the slide show would be shown at a gathering of his friends at a memorial service. Who could have imagined that such a young spirit would fall so early to leukemia? He was gone within two years of making the trip. Don Bell, professor of history at the University of Washington, the leader of the delegation—such a generous and welcoming man—taken by the Lord ("*Absalom, Absalom*," cried the letter from his wife informing us of his passing) within a few years of the event.

And the rest of you—how did the trip to the USSR impact your lives? Looking forward to learning the rest of the story.

Media That Matters at KING-TV5, Seattle, Washington, 1985—1990, by Anne Stadler. In Anne's essay we read about an extraordinary bridge between two "enemy" cultures. This space bridge provided by television, engaged people in two worlds simultaneously through many kinds of programs. Over a five-year period, Anne Stadler and Jean Enerson participated in two Spacebridges with the USSR, documentaries, made appearances on each other's programs, news reports & exchanges, and audience participation programs. For people of the twenty-first century, it is hard to imagine how bold it was for two television hosts to bring their audiences together across the Iron Curtain in 1985.

Media That Matters at KING-TV5 Seattle, Washington, 1985 - 1990

By Anne Stadler and Jean Enersen
Seattle, Washington, 1985:

We were living in a bipolar world. Every school child in the United States was taught that the Soviet Union was a dangerous enemy who could cause nuclear war. The policy of mutual assured destruction governed security relationships between the United States and the Soviet Union, the world's two great powers. This relationship had been relatively stable since the early '50s.

But there were changes happening. There were signs in the Soviet Union that the Soviet communist system was not able to support its "Great Power" status. The arms race and a stagnant official economic life were dragging it down. A second economy of barter and favors was increasingly evident—its vitality essential to the lives of ordinary citizens.

So, at the 1986 Party Congress, Mikhail Gorbachev announced two new policies: *glasnost* to open up the social and political system, and *perestroika* to open up the economy and generate new economic development.

In the US, President Reagan and his advisors were shifting US policy to take advantage of the cracks in the Soviet monolith.

Seattle, with its concentration on aircraft and defense manufacturing and its nearby military installations, was a target of Soviet missiles and nuclear warheads. There was high community interest in learning about relations between our country and the Soviet Union. People of different political persuasions shared the feeling that the best way to deal with the possible Soviet threat was to get to know them. As one person said: "Keep friends close. Keep enemies even closer."

Target Seattle was a major eruption of citizen activism aimed at understanding the nature of our enemy and preventing war.

Our station, KING-TV5, was very much involved in pioneering interactive television with a broad-based citizen coalition called People Power. From 1978 to 1983, Anne Stadler and Jean Enersen worked on programs about national and international security with People Power, first on *Classified Critical*, an award-winning series of programs about the arms race and national security, and later on Target Seattle.

During that time, Anne Stadler had participated in experiments bringing people face-to-face using slow-scan television and she began to investigate broadcast television being used to bring people face-to-face via satellite transmission. She imagined doing a televised space bridge between citizens of Seattle and a city in the Soviet Union, so people could actually talk directly with one another. Several times she proposed the project to KING-TV5 officials, but the timing wasn't right.

Television Brings US and Soviet Citizens Face-to-Face:

In December 1985, KING-TV5 broadcast the first US-USSR space bridge. Moderated by Phil Donahue and Vladimir Posner, United States' and Soviet citizens talked directly to each other about their daily lives. And audiences in both countries were witnesses.

By the end of 1986, a team from News and Programming was in the Soviet Union filming *Face to Face*, a documentary coproduced with Soviet television. Our goal was to meet the enemy face-to-face, to learn more about how they lived, what their homes looked like, where they shopped, what they did for fun, what the circumstances of their work were. We followed two citizens who met on the space bridge: Andrei Yakovlev, a Soviet artist, and Rob Morrow, a high school teacher from Kent, Washington.

For both production teams, this was a first: the first time a Soviet TV crew had videotaped the mundane details of daily life in the United States; the first time Americans saw the mundane details of Soviet family life. A subtext of the documentary was the working experience our two crews had.

ANNE:

Before the first shoot, our two production teams had breakfast together, Pavel Korchagin, one of the Soviet Producers, made a joking comment about how we couldn't trust them. And I realized, yes, that's exactly how I do feel. So I decided I needed to bring that into the open, and to establish an authentic ground rule for our work together.

I asked Pavel and his colleague, Sergei Skvortsov, to meet me before we went out on the shoot. I told them: "I'm not here to be a mouthpiece for our government. I want to find out what it's like to live here and to tell the truth about what I find out. And I want you to do the same. Will you commit to doing that?" After a surprised and somewhat embarrassed pause, they agreed.

I realize this may sound absurd, since neither of us could tell if the others were lying. But I knew I would keep my word. As it turned out, this was a commitment we honored throughout all of our work together.

JEAN:

I was born curious. And I was a skeptic. We had done plenty of stories about what the Soviet threat was. So, given what we'd learned during Target Seattle, I felt they might be as afraid of mutual assured destruction as we were. The space bridge opened up a small window of conversation. I figured we could either sit here, or we could go and find out who they are and what the threat really is.

So, throughout our whole trip all of us kept our eyes open. Could we trust them? Are we and they a team? Is it possible to *be* a team? What are we actually seeing? And how representative is it?

Fortunately, Anne found several Seattle contacts who knew people and places in Leningrad and Moscow—and our NBC colleagues proved really helpful as well. They gave us independent ideas and connections on where to film and what to look for—so we weren't entirely dependent on our Soviet producers.

After *Face to Face*, KING-TV5 continued to do joint programming with Soviet TV. Anne was coordinating producer for eleven coproduction broadcast projects, six of which were shown in both countries. Several of our programs were shown in the Soviet Union just before major historic events were announced. *Teen Bridge: US/*

USSR (with young people from Seattle and Leningrad) aired just before the INF Treaty announcement. It was moderated at our end by Jean Enersen.

In another first, Jean was on the air live for a week on Soviet television. And a reciprocal agreement had Yevgeny Kiselev live on KING-TV5 for a week. Their stories were aired in both countries. Later, a Donahue-style series on American life moderated by Vladimir Posner aired just before the Moscow Summit between Ronald Reagan and Mikhail Gorbachev.

During this period, we had another experience of being face-to-face: we often found ourselves face-to-face with our own stereotypes.

JEAN:

We had continuing conversations about censorship. They openly acknowledged that their job was to tell the story their government wanted to be told. We felt we were free to observe and then report what we saw.

One evening, Sergei reminded me forcefully and playfully that in fact we did practice a kind of censorship: internal censorship, noticing some things which our peers and viewers would accept and not noticing others. There's a wonderful snapshot of him and me with gaffer tape over my mouth to illustrate his point.

ANNE:

Another occasion happened in Moscow during our weeklong series of live appearances on Soviet television. Each day, Jean Enersen did a story on a feature of Soviet life. We edited it and it aired the next day, with Jean talking for about fifteen minutes after the story with Soviet anchor Yevgeny Kiselov.

We had shot and were editing a piece about Afghan veterans and their similarities to American veterans of the Vietnam war, when our Soviet colleagues told us their boss said we couldn't air the piece. We had an agreement that there would be no censorship, and that had been honored meticulously, so this news precipitated a real crisis. We sat with our Soviet colleagues, discussing very frankly our differing points of view. They would then transmit our conversation to their boss, Valentin Lazutkin, the head of Gosteleradio.

Finally, we were all summoned to meet with him. He told us: "The Soviet people have not yet been told about the Afghan war (it had been presented as a policing action), the situation of Afghan veterans, or that they are experiencing any difficulties. It would be unseemly and wrong for you to be the first to announce this to our citizens. This is why we ask you to withdraw the story."

We considered this and agreed that was a reasonable request *and* declared we wanted to tell the story of what had happened to both audiences. He agreed. So, we did that. Jean told Soviet viewers about the story which had not been shown. And, on the KING-TV5 broadcast, she also interviewed Pavel Korchagin discussing why the Afghan story had not aired.

The Results:

The benefits were legion. In the narrowest view, our corporation KING Broadcasting benefited. KING-TV5's marketing identity reflected our commitment to this kind of programming.

The programs attracted sizable audiences and corporate sponsors, contributing to our economic welfare. *Face to Face* was the most popular locally-produced documentary in our history. It drew the biggest audience and won many awards.

Our community benefited. It has since become one of the nodes of economic and cultural cooperation between countries of the former Soviet Union and the United States.

Our colleagues in KING-TV5 benefited—from the receptionist to the telex operator, the production teams, the reporters, the owners—all of us had the immense thrill of being part of the vast changes that were happening between us and our "enemy."

Many of us had the unusual experience of alignment between our own personal purpose in the world and one of the great moments in history. At a crucial transition time in the history of US-Soviet relations, we were having conversations with our Soviet colleagues about the nature of press freedom; how, as reporters, we tried to maintain a mental stance of including all the diversity present in any situation; asking each other what does it mean to tell the truth? We were each doing programming which influenced the perceptions of our audiences toward each other's countries. And right from the start of our working relationships, we were consciously committed to telling the truth and living the practice of friendship.

There Were Many Wonderful Moments!

JEAN :

We were walking along looking for some shopping opportunities in Leningrad. Anne and our interpreter were a little ahead of me. A young man fell in beside me saying he wanted to practice his English. Could he walk along with me and prove it?

He was wearing blue jeans and running shoes with an American label. He looked more American than a lot of Americans. After some preliminary conversation he came out with "How about meeting me at the Pushkin statue tonight and I'll show you I can make love like an American."

In the end, we're all interested in the same thing!

ANNE:

In 1988, when I was in Tashkent, Uzbekistan, I attended a lunch with American women and Uzbek women. The Uzbeks were asking a lot of questions about our lives. Several times they prefaced their questions with "I saw that some American women do X, could you tell us more about that?"

Finally, I asked: "Where did you see this information?"

"We saw it on television," they replied, "There were a whole group of American women talking with Vladimir Posner. It was part of a series of programs."

I was amazed! Here was direct evidence of how "Our" programming contributed to the awareness of viewers in the Soviet Union.

At KING Broadcasting's forty-fifth anniversary, CEO. Ancil Payne told us that one of our founder's basic precepts was "Work is love made visible." We lived that as we did this work. And our efforts demonstrated television used at its highest purpose.

Richard (Dick) Carter and his wife, Jane, provide an example of the many deep, personal friendships that developed across cultures because of Target Seattle. In Carter's essay *Andrei Yakovlev—A Memorial*, he describes the specific connection created by the KING-TV5 television Spacebridge that resulted in his twenty-five-year friendship with the Russian artist, Yakovlev. His tender reflection invites the reader to seek a similar opportunity, to find his or her own deep friendship across borders.

Andrei Yakovlev—A Memorial

By Richard Carter
Edited by Jane Carter

My friend of twenty-five years, Andrei Yakovlev of St. Petersburg, Russia, died in 2012. News of his death prompted me to write this memorial, not only to his life but to the friendship that existed between us. Even though he is no longer with us, we will always be friends in my heart and mind. This will be a description of that friendship.

If it hadn't been for Rob Morrow at Highline High School, I never would have met Andrei Yakovlev. Rob was a student in one of the Spanish classes I taught at Highline High School. He grew up to become the principal at Mt. Tahoma High School. In 1985, several years after he graduated from Highline, Rob was in the studio audience when Phil Donahue, working with KING-TV5, presented a sky bridge [space bridge] between Seattle and Leningrad (now Saint Petersburg). Vladimir Pozner was the emcee in Leningrad. Audiences in the two cities were able to talk to one another via television.

Andrei Yakovlev, a well-known contemporary Russian artist, was in the audience in Leningrad. He had gained fame and popularity by living among, and doing portraits of, the natives of the Chukchi tribe across the Bering Strait from Alaska. He had also traveled with and painted reindeer herders in northern Siberia and had done portraits of railroad construction workers building a new line across Siberia. His paintings were displayed in the Tretyakov Gallery in Moscow and in the Russian Museum in Leningrad.

During the TV show, Andrei said the Americans had "interesting faces," and that he would like to paint them. The people at KING-TV5 took up his idea and invited him to Seattle to do that. While visiting

Seattle, he did a portrait of Rob and they became friends. He even stayed with Rob and his wife. His visit to the high school where Rob was teaching was one of the highlights of his stay in the Seattle area. Then in 1986, Rob visited Andrei in Leningrad.

Jean Enersen, the news anchor at KING-TV5, along with a camera crew, went there to film the visit. The TV documentary was called *Face to Face* and it was shown in both countries shortly afterwards.

I came into the picture in 1987. I had won a six-week government fellowship given to American teachers of Russian. A group of twenty-five of us were attending the Herzen Language Institute in Leningrad to improve our Russian language skills. While we were there, a group of twenty-five Russian teachers of English were having a parallel experience in Philadelphia. In talking to Rob, I found out that he was planning to be in Leningrad visiting Andrei at the same time that I would be there. "Good," I thought to myself, "maybe I'll get to meet Andrei." However, when I arrived at the institute, there was a message for me from Rob. He had had to leave for home a couple days sooner than expected. I said to myself, "there goes my chance to meet Andrei."

The first morning I was there, I walked the two blocks up to Leningrad's main street, the Nevsky Prospect, to buy a morning newspaper. I turned away from the kiosk and came face-to-face with Andrei. He lived only about two blocks off the Nevsky Prospect on its opposite side from me. He was out walking his little gray poodle, Tyunya. He didn't know me, of course, but I recognized him from having seen him on TV. I introduced myself and told him of my connection with Rob Morrow. He gave me a big smile and said, in effect, "any friend of Rob Morrow's is a friend of mine." Then, in the course of our conversation, he invited me to come to dinner and meet his wife, Larisa. That was the beginning of our long friendship.

Andrei was in his early fifties and had what I consider a typical Slavic face: slightly high cheekbones, a well-proportioned nose, and regular features that easily broke into a smile. He was about my height with a slim build and a vigorous manner of moving. The cool weather and his walks helped keep his complexion ruddy—especially noticeable when he remembered to shave.

On my first visit to his apartment, Andrei took me next door to show me his studio. His apartment and his studio were separated by an alley. From his apartment you had to take an elevator down to the ground floor, walk next door, then take another elevator up to his studio. The studio was like a set in the opera *La Boheme*. It was on the top floor of a four-story building and the ceiling was a large area of glass to let in lots of natural light. His painter's easel dominated the middle of the room. Half-finished paintings and stretched, framed canvasses were scattered around the walls. At the east end of the room there was a bed covered with a multicolored quilt. He liked to rest there when he was on a big project. A grand piano stood at the other end of the large room. There was a toilet in a small booth off the hallway leading to the studio. The never-cleaned toilet barely worked and was in such bad shape that Andrei called it a "national disaster."

While we were touring the studio, Larisa was fixing dinner. She was very Russian looking: round face, button nose, rosy cheeks, slightly overweight, and had a perpetual smile. Larisa was a curator at the Russian Museum and she had met Andrei in the course of her work there. As his soul mate, she gave Andrei inspiration, guidance, and stability.

First there was vodka. All the meals at the Yakovlevs' were preceded and accompanied by lots of vodka. During the vodka course, we enjoyed talking about our mutual acquaintances in Seattle and about life in general. He and Larisa were very interested in the fact that I had an adopted son. Adoption was not unknown in Russia, it simply was not publicized. The big question was whether or not to tell the child and all your friends and relatives that the child was adopted. The Yakovlevs had a young friend named Sasha who had grown up in an orphanage. This gave them an interest in orphans and orphanages.

Andrei and Larisa also wanted to know all about the exchange program which had brought me to Russia. Talking about that got us into talking about literature, politics, history, and whatever. I think that was when I first heard Andrei say in his highly accented English, "Hitler, Stalin, fifty-fifty." In the course of the conversation we found that we were in such close agreement that Andrei said, "The politicians should put us in charge. We could solve all their problems." Also in the course of the meal, Andrei suggested that we use the familiar instead of the formal form of address. This is a big deal in Russian because it not only changes the word for *you*, it also changes all the verb forms.

But best of all, it puts you on a true-friend or family relationship level.

Dinner was an elaborate, two-hour treat. Throughout the meal there was vodka, Pepsi Cola, and tea. There was also your choice of bread, French or Russian black bread. The first course was a salad, basically cucumber and tomato, but heavily garnished with cilantro, fresh dill, and basil. As part of the salad course we had fish: smoked sturgeon and lox. The main course was a beef cutlet served with peas and a peeled, baked potato. This was followed by what might be called the cheese course. On the tray were various kinds of cheeses along with dill pickles and black olives. Dessert was freshly-baked layer cake—moist and soft with a half-inch layer of frosting. After eating our fills, we lingered over coffee while Tyunya entertained us with his tricks: rolling over, walking on his hind legs, catching a ball, shaking hands, and turning flips in midair. It was truly a dinner to remember.

Over the next four weeks there were several such dinners. Strangely, the most memorable was the dinner on the night before my group left Leningrad to stay in Moscow a few days. Larisa served *pelmeni*. Pelmeni are like ravioli: a tasty meat filling wrapped in dough, then cooked in chicken broth. They're served with a big dollop of sour cream and soy sauce for seasoning. Larisa kept refilling my plate. Finally, on the third plateful I had to admit that I could eat no more. Andrei, Larisa, and Tyunya walked me back to the institute where a bus was waiting. My roommate had brought my baggage down and I was one of the last to board. When I said goodbye, I knew that we would meet again.

When I returned with Jane in 1990, Andrei's helpfulness and kindness were unsurpassed. That was when I heard Andrei say the only other phrase in English that he knew, "You are beautiful. I luf you." We were with a group of high school students on a two-week exchange program with School No. 70. For the first week, we stayed with one of the teachers, Irina Larionova. We moved in with the Yakovlevs for the second week. It was further from the school so Andrei had to go to great lengths to find taxis for us. On the first day of our stay with him he went with us in the taxi so we would know where to meet at the end of the school day. We could have taken public transportation but he insisted on arranging cabs for us.

The most lasting memento of that visit is a portrait of Jane. She sat for the portrait almost every day in the week we were there. While he was doing the busy work of painting, he talked Jane into playing the piano. At one point he thought he might have the portrait finished and Larisa told him to leave it alone. But then he decided to "make it better," and in tinkering with it he lost Jane's expression. This distressed him no end, and he took it back to the studio. Eventually it came out perfect. It will always hang in a prominent place in our home. The painting is such an exact likeness of her that some people think it is a photograph.

Another major event of that visit was when Andrei invited all fourteen of my students to visit his studio and apartment. For most of them it was the first time they had ever seen an artist's studio. With me translating, he described the projects he was working on, how the lighting was so important, and how he prepared his canvasses for painting. After touring the studio, we went back to his apartment. It was a very Russian apartment and certainly unlike anything my students had ever seen. Most of the furniture was antique from the early nineteenth century. Andrei and Larisa, like most Russians, were great admirers of the poet Alexander Pushkin. Their choice of furniture was all from the era when Pushkin lived. The walls were covered with paintings and drawings—most of them done by Andrei. A huge full-length portrait of an unknown aristocrat of the nineteenth century dominated one end of the room. At the other end of that main room, beyond a table and the icon corner, there were windows looking out onto a department store across the street.

After my students left and while we were having tea, Sasha came to visit. He was a mild-mannered, pleasant young man in his twenties with blond hair and handsome features. He spoke fairly good English, so Jane enjoyed talking to him. Sasha's full name was Alexander Tsygankov and he played an important role in the lives of Andrei and Larisa. They had met when Sasha was just out of the army and was working as a carpenter. He had come to Andrei's studio to install a door. In the course of his work they became acquainted and he became a lifelong friend of the Yakovlevs. They always treated him as a member of the family. Sasha was the young man I mentioned earlier who had grown up in an orphanage.

In 1997 Andrei and Larisa went to Austria and Italy. Andrei was painting and selling pictures to pay for their trip. While staying in Vienna, Andrei and Larisa had their marriage blessed by the Orthodox Church. The Soviet Union had collapsed in 1991 and the new government took on more friendly relations with the church. There was no longer a stigma attached to being a Christian. Andrei and Larisa started attending services in Saint Petersburg and wanted their union to be blessed by the church. During their trip to Europe it seemed like the perfect time and place to have it done.

When we visited them in their apartment, Larisa always outdid herself in setting a bountiful table. Sometimes it was just us at dinner, but often there were other friends. The friends were sometimes art buyers, sometimes artists, but more often they were workers and directors of art museums. In 2006 there was an especially gala affair. The day of the dinner party, the mayor of Saint Petersburg had presented Andrei a gold medal for outstanding artistic achievement. The medal came from the president, Vladimir Putin, and it had been presented to Andrei at the Smolny Institute. Jane and I didn't find out until we arrived that we had been invited to share in the celebration. At one point, Andrei dipped the medal in his vodka, then passed it around so everyone could do the same. When the medal had bestowed its spirit into everyone's spirits, we toasted Andrei's reward.

Sometimes when Jane and I didn't get to see Andrei and Larisa it was because it was summer and they were at their dacha in the village of Pavshino, almost one hundred miles south of Saint Petersburg. Andrei spent most of his time painting landscapes inspired by the countryside. Getting to the dacha was no small task. The first leg of the journey was by train, then they took a bus to the end of the line, then they walked a few miles to the bank of a river. They had to ring a bell or yell until a neighbor in their small village came across the river in a rowboat to pick them up. Coming back to Saint Petersburg was just the reverse of that journey. Jane and I never went there, but Andrei gave us six of his paintings of the dacha and its surroundings as it looked during different seasons of the year.

There was a time in 2003 when Andrei made that trip just for Jane and me. We were in Saint Petersburg on some church business and on a free evening we called to see if the Yakovlevs were home. Larisa was at the apartment, but Andrei was at the dacha. Larisa urged us to come visit even without Andrei because she looked forward to seeing us. Jane and I accepted the invitation and enjoyed the usual pleasant visit. At the end of the meal the apartment door opened and in walked Andrei. There were shouts of joy and lots of hugs. Andrei gave only vague answers when asked how he had found out about our visit. I suspect that someone in or near his village had a telephone and somehow word of our visit had gotten to him.

Between 2006 and 2010 we didn't go to Russia. In February 2010 we went back to Saint Petersburg with a delegation sponsored by the Russian Orthodox Church. We found Andrei in deep grief over the death of Larisa. Sasha Tsygankov helped Andrei prepare a dinner for us. We learned that Larisa had died of cancer in 2009. Andrei had staged an art exhibit in her honor, which featured paintings from their happy times at the dacha. The centerpiece of the exhibit was a large painting that will always haunt me as an expression of sorrow. His beloved dog, Tyunya, who had died several years previously, was sitting next to a large, blank canvas. A small yellow butterfly has landed on the canvas. Andrei pointed out that the butterfly was the soul of Larisa. I couldn't hold back my tears. We spent most of that evening watching movies of the happy times that they had spent at their dacha. It didn't occur to us that this might be the last time we were to see Andrei.

Sasha had email, but like many Russians, he was slow in responding to my messages. Consequently, there was no news from Saint Petersburg in almost two years. Jane and I kept hoping that Andrei had recovered from his grief and was keeping himself busy with his artwork. Finally, in September of 2012, curiosity prompted me to call Andrei's number. Sasha answered. It seems that Andrei had died in June and Sasha had inherited the apartment. Andrei had been getting ready for a trip to Pavshino to fix up the dacha and do more painting. On June 13, Sasha got a phone call from him. All he said was, "I'm short of breath. I'm dying." It took Sasha 20 minutes to rush over to him. By the time he arrived, Andrei had indeed died. Maybe we can all be lucky enough to die as quietly.

When I first started learning the Russian language, I dreamed of meeting an ordinary Russian citizen and convincing him/her that Americans were not the war-mongering gangsters that the Communist government made us out to be. Andrei was not an ordinary citizen, and he didn't need to be convinced about the goodness of Americans.

However, having him as a friend rewarded me for my years of studying the language and it fulfilled my desire to have a friend in Russia

In Memory of Larisa Yakovlev

Acknowledgments

Several years ago, I picked up Natalie Goldberg's book about memoir "Old Friend from Far Away." Attending several of her residential writing practice workshops slowed me down enough to listen, peel away the layers and find my authentic voice. Because of Natalie, I found others to write with and have learned from their voices, spoken aloud at the tables in coffee shops in Seattle. She taught me to pick up the pen, open the notebook, set the timer and write as a daily practice. As I read more, "The Art of Memoir," "Liar's Club," and "Lit" by Mary Karr became beacons that guided me.

Stacks of filled notebooks later, I needed to learn the craft of pulling scenes together into a good story. I enrolled in Scott Driscoll's Professional Fiction Writing year-long class at the University of Washington. I will never again read a short story, novel, essay or watch a movie without an awareness of the dramatic arc. After several more of his off-campus classes, I felt I had something worth reading in "Open Borders."

Louis Whitford edited my story, working with me to develop the story arc and then line edited my manuscript, teaching me along the way. He has helped me transition from writer to author.

I am especially grateful to Virginia McDermott, co-leader with my husband of our travel group in March of 1983. Her generous insight through several readings has made my story much stronger.

Thanks also to Roscius Doan, Kay Bullitt, Ruth Bell, and Masha Reichert all of whom were on the trip, for their encouragement, for reading the early drafts and helping recall details of our travels. And to Fred Noland and Jim Halfaker, fellow travelers, for cheering me on in this effort.

Cabby Tennis' careful reading and comments were a gift.

Jennifer McCord, who co-taught a class with Driscoll and serves both as a self-publisher's project manager and editor for Coffeetown Press, saw something in my story and encouraged me to see it through to completion.

Marlow Boyer, artist and creator of the *City to City, People to People* multimedia show, gave the world a pictorial record of people studying alternatives to war, gathering courage and traveling behind enemy lines to find common ground with people on the other side. His images inspired me, over and over, as I presented them to audience after audience, reinforcing my belief that the best way to peace in our world is through friendship. I have made every attempt to locate the curators of his estate to obtain permission to use his photographs in this book. They have been in my possession for the past thirty-four years. I took responsibility for transferring the show faithfully, just as he created it, to a digital DVD format. Marlow and David Boyer, his father, created an edited version with the support of the National Geographic just a month before Marlow died.

Shelley Brubaker, who helped develop the show, partnered with me on the east coast tour and presented Marlow's work across Washington State. Without her, none of us would have been able to tell the Target Seattle story to so many.

My daughters have supported my writing, cheered me on, read drafts and reminded me of their whereabouts during this period.

I am grateful to all my fellow travelers in March of 1983: Marlow Boyer, Kay Bullitt, John Burhop, Tory Campbell, Paul Cooke, Rosh and Joyce Doan, Kathleen Braden, Lucy Dougall, Sara Fleming, Jim Halfaker, Jon Halfaker, Craig Justice, Nora Leech, Nick Licata, Carmen Matthews, Raymond Nielsen, Masha Reichert, Jean Rolfe, Nick Rothenberg, Bill Sieverling, Virginia Stout, Hugh and Linda Straley and Rachel Straley, Stam Bradley, Roy and Maryanne Wiebe, and Connie Youel.

ABOUT THE AUTHORS

Photo by Drew Rose

Betsy Bell is a high-energy grandma to fifteen young adult grandchildren, a political activist, business owner, and author. She has published several poems and two memoir pieces in various journals. Passionate about physical well-being, she hikes, cross-country skis, dances, gardens, and walks or rides the bus when possible.

ROSCIUS DOAN IS A RETIRED physician. Rosh first traveled to Tashkent in March 1983. In 1987, he helped found a Medical Exchange Program in Tashkent. Out of this came subsequent trips focusing on public health, virology, epidemiology, emergency medicine, and the Peace Park Project. In 1990, he lived for a year in Tashkent with his wife Joyce and daughter Marisha.

CRAIG JUSTICE IS VICE PRESIDENT WORLDWIDE Sales for The HoverCam and founder of Keizai Society. His specialty is accelerating revenue worldwide through effective channel management and business development. Justice traveled to Tashkent in 1983 as a journalist.

ANNE STADLER WAS THE AMERICAN co-producer of King-TV5's programming with Gosteleradio (Soviet TV & radio) from 1986-1990. She worked with Jean Enersen and other KING-TV5 staff on a number of award-winning programs.

RICHARD CARTER, RETIRED TEACHER OF Spanish and Russian, befriended the Russian artist Andrei Yakovlev. They exchanged many visits to each other's homeland over twenty-five years.

Open Borders
Topics for Discussion

Open Borders tells the story of direct conversations between citizens of two nations considered hostile to each other. The intent was to break down walls between nations.

- How do you view this type of action in the current political environment?
- How do social media interactions compare to face-to-face conversations?
- Do you believe the actions taken were effective in furthering peace?

Nationalism and ethnic isolation are on the rise around the world. The author advocates freedom of movement across international boundaries and the vital importance of human connections between citizens of different nations.

- In our current political environment what challenges do you see to this approach?
- What nations would you put at the top of your list for organized civilian action?
- Would terrorism and personal safety issues prevent you from visiting Russia? Iran? North Korea?
- Do you see value in isolating another nation?

Like many women of that time, the author struggles with her role as a wife and a mother and her desire to have a career.

- Many more women work outside of the home today, but is this challenge a thing of the past?

- Have you or someone you know struggled with similar issues?

Moral purpose guides the author and her husband as they become deeply involved in the local efforts to reduce the nuclear threat between the Soviet Union and the United States.

- What principles guide you?
- Have your principals driven you to unexpected social or political action?
- How have you responded when a principled action puts you into conflict with someone you respect?
- How might you resolve those differences?